Contents

What Has New Labour Done for Primary Care?

A balance sheet

Edited by Stephen Gillam

Foreword by Rudolf Klein

Published by
King's Fund Publishing
11–13 Cavendish Square
London W1G 0AN

© King's Fund 2001

First published 2001

ISBN 1 85717 445 3

A CIP catalogue record for this book is available from the British Library

Available from:
King's Fund Bookshop
11–13 Cavendish Square
LONDON
W1G 0AN

Tel: 020 7307 2591
Fax: 020 7307 2801

Printed and bound in Great Britain

Cover photographs: Robert Aberman and Department of Health

Foreword

One of the characteristics of New Labour's first term in office has been the restless, insistent proliferation of new initiatives. The NHS is no exception and indeed has become a laboratory of change. Its landscape appears to be constantly shifting as ministerial announcements follow each other with bewildering frequency. This is as true of primary care as of the rest of the service. The rhetoric of a primary care-led NHS – inherited from the Conservative government – has been translated into action. Not only has fundholding been universalised in the shape of primary care groups, but NHS Direct and walk-in health centres have been launched. Hence the value of this analysis that examines the impact – actual and, more important, potential – of the various initiatives and seeks to put them into the wider context of the other changes in the NHS. It thus offers a guide both to those directly involved in primary care and to those concerned more generally about the future of health care delivery in this country.

The questions that shape the analysis provide a checklist against which not only progress so far but also future achievement can be assessed. Will the changes improve access and quality? And are these two policy goals necessarily compatible or may some of the policy tools designed to improve access put quality at risk? Will the input of resources – managerial as well as professional – match the new demands being made on primary care? Can primary care groups (PCGs), as they evolve into new primary care trusts (PCTs), succeed in bridging the divide between health and social services? How will general practitioners, heirs to a long tradition of individualism, adapt to a new environment that requires them, in effect, to police each other? Is there a danger of regulatory overload as clinical governance, revalidation and visitations from the Commission for Health Improvement impose extra burdens on the resources (and time) of those engaged in actually delivering primary care? And how can the competing demands of upward accountability for delivering national policy goals and targets be reconciled with downward accountability to consumers?

No definite answers can as yet be given to any of these questions. As the various contributions to this analysis make clear, the changes are only slowly working themselves through the system. And, as always in the NHS, there are wide variations in the way they are being implemented: in the capacity, commitment and enthusiasm of those involved. What is clear from the analysis, however, is that the changes will challenge many of our basic assumptions about primary care and, similarly, about what it means to be a professional: for example, the way we think about the roles of doctors and nurses. In short, the prospect is both exciting and unsettling: we are moving into a future that is inventing itself and where it is difficult to predict the eventual outcome.

So we come to what is perhaps the most important question: how ministers will react to what will inevitably be an untidy process, as change springs surprises that reveal both new opportunities and new problems. Will they seek to discipline variation by imposing national models? Or will they welcome diversity and accept that there are different ways of achieving their policy goals? The hope must be that flexibility will win out. The initiatives reviewed in this analysis are best seen as experiments. And it will take time to come to any definitive conclusions about which of them work. So much will depend on whether or not ministers can resist the temptation of trying to short-circuit the process, and whether or not they have the patience and stamina to settle for the long haul. Perhaps the answer is a moratorium on new initiatives.

Rudolf Klein

Introduction

The policy pre-occupations of successive governments over the last 20 years have been consistent: containing costs and increasing efficiency, addressing variations in clinical quality, increasing professional accountability, improving access and user responsiveness. The Conservatives introduced reforms in 1990 that concentrated on controlling costs and quality through the introduction of an internal market.[1] A central policy instrument was fundholding, which capitalised on general practitioners' intimate knowledge of local services (derived from their traditional 'gate-keeping' function) and their financial entrepreneurialism (derived from their traditional autonomy as independent contractors). If the previous decade had been one of unparalleled turbulence in the NHS, any expectations that the pace of change might slow with a change of government were soon to be discarded. As New Labour's ten-year 'project' approaches a possible halfway point, what can we say about progress to date?

This monograph begins by considering New Labour's inheritance and goes on to chronicle key reforms inaugurated since 1997 (Table 1.2). It takes stock of achievements in addressing the same policy imperatives listed above and looks ahead at the likely impact of changes proposed in *The NHS Plan*.[2] Central for policy analysts – if not for practitioners or the public – were the overhaul of the internal market and the formation of primary care groups (PCGs).

In the second chapter, Dominique Florin examines the meaning of access to the service and recent attempts to extend it. Some commentators argue that this government has begun to tamper dangerously with what is right, as well as with what is wrong, with primary care:[3] for example, that health outcomes may be impaired if the establishment of free-standing emergency centres compromises continuity of personal care.[4]

Labour's was allegedly a ten-year project, but the development of effective primary care trusts (PCTs) was always going to take more time than the electoral cycle allowed. Similarly, the implementation of clinical governance was never going to keep health scandals from the national news. In Chapter 3, Rebecca Rosen asks whether this latest system-wide initiative is likely to have improved the quality of care.

Even without the more lurid events of the last four years, renegotiation of the relationship between the NHS monolith, those who work with it and those it serves was likely to be the most difficult challenge facing a new administration. Will Anderson explores the ambiguous, consumerist nature of new initiatives to involve the public in Chapter 4.

There are risks in abandoning too hastily the infamous 'red book', which has proved a durable mechanism for the central direction of general practice. New payment systems could prove less flexible with higher transaction costs.[5] The implications of recent developments for the national contract are discussed by Richard Lewis in Chapter 5, where he considers the changing nature of accountability in general practice. He looks also at the new forms of accountability GPs must face as commissioners of care.

Prime ministerial frustration at the slow pace of modernisation was understandable. The concluding chapter looks beyond *The*

NHS Plan in a critical summary of progress to date. The contributions form a sequence but also stand alone. The policy perspectives and themes chosen for scrutiny are necessarily selective. In particular, the focus is on England. The new primary care organisations evolving in other parts of the United Kingdom will provide intriguing material for future comparative analysis. Nonetheless, these essays illustrate the breadth of change – the sweep of this government's aspirations for primary care and, in particular, for general practice. Not-so-new Labour is worth a second term, but could yet break the NHS under the weight of its good intentions.

Stephen Gillam

References

[1] Secretary of State for Health. *Working for patients.* London: HMSO, Cm 555.78, 1989.

[2] NHS Executive. *The NHS Plan. A plan for investment. A plan for reform.* London: The Stationery Office, Cm 4818-I, 2000.

[3] De Maeseneer J, Hjortdahl P, Starfield B. Fix what's wrong, not what's right, with general practice in Britain. *BMJ* 2000; 320: 1616–67.

[4] Starfield B. *Primary care: balancing health needs, services and technology.* Oxford: Oxford University Press, 1998.

[5] Lewis R, Gillam S. What seems to be the trouble? *Health Services Journal* 2000; 27 July.

Chapter 1: Perpetual evolution: a stocktake

Stephen Gillam

The inheritance

Fundholding came to be seen as the spearhead of a 'primary care-led NHS'.[1] Although its champions claimed great benefits from the scheme, the evidence to support these claims is equivocal. The Audit Commission concluded that most fundholding practices had produced only modest improvements, which were probably insufficient to justify their higher cost.[2] Fundholding spawned a variety of attempts to adopt a more comprehensive and integrated approach to health care, including total purchasing, multi-funds and locality commissioning. Each in their different ways recognised a need to plan and budget for comprehensive provision, usually for populations considerably larger than the average general practice. Despite the continued emphasis on the role of general practice in purchasing hospital and community services, the evidence from the evaluation of total purchasing suggested that the most sites were at least as concerned to develop primary care services.[3]

Ultimately, fundholding was unsuccessful in several respects.[4] It was bureaucratic, involving high transaction costs. It was perceived as unfair: fundholders generated inequities in access to care ('two-tierism'). It was difficult to demonstrate that general practitioners were effective or impartial as advocates in their patients' interests. Most importantly, the internal market failed to deliver anticipated efficiency gains. Yet, fundholding did entrench political support for widening the involvement of general practitioners in resource allocation and service planning.

Transitional objects – the curious place of PMS

General medical services (GMS) and general practice as provider of services were left otherwise untouched by the internal market. A new contract was imposed in 1990. It provided tools to increase the accountability of GPs but failed to address deep-rooted deficits in primary care, and was criticised for its lack of local flexibility. This was a central theme emerging from then minister Gerald Malone's appeasement offensive: the 'Listening Exercise' of 1995.

The *Choice and opportunity* White Paper of the same year was in many ways a response to pressure for change from within the medical profession.[5] The General Medical Services Committee of the BMA was seeking to renegotiate the compulsory contractual requirement of 24-hour responsibility for care and to define more tightly the nature of 'core' general medical services. Recruitment and retention of doctors was problematic, and there were many indications that a growing minority of GPs were seeking salaried or alternative employment options.[6]

The NHS (Primary Care) Act 1997 – passed in the dying days of the *ancien regime* – nevertheless marked a revolutionary change.[7] The launch of personal medical services (PMS) pilot schemes marked the ending of GPs' monopoly of primary medical care, with new market entrants in the shape of NHS trusts and nurses. The long-cherished national contract was no longer to apply universally with the development of alternative employment options to that of the independent GMS/GDS contractor. However, the priority attached to this part of their inheritance by the new ministerial team was initially unclear.

Table 1.1: Chronology of events

April 1997	*The NHS Primary Care Act* passed
May 1997	New Labour government elected
December 1997	*The new NHS: modern, dependable* published
April 1998	85 first wave PMS pilots go live
June 1998	*A first class service* published
August 1998	Beacon practices announced
March 1999	First NHS Direct pilot evaluation reported
April 1999	PCGs go live
April 1999	20 first wave walk-in centres announced
May 1999	Frank Dobson announces restrictions on Viagra prescribing
October 1999	NICE publishes first recommendation on Relenza
October 1999	Second wave PMS pilots go live
November 1999	First healthy living centres launched
November 1999	*Supporting doctors, protecting patients* published
December 1999	Coverage of NHS Direct extends across the country
January 2000	Harold Shipman convicted
February 2000	Commission for Health Improvement launched
April 2000	17 first wave primary care trusts go live
May 2000	Third wave of PMS pilots announced for April 2001 – up to 25% of GPs subsequently express interest
July 2000	*The NHS Plan* published

The new NHS

The publication of the Labour government's White Paper *The new NHS: modern, dependable*[8] formally announced the demise of GP fundholding and the internal market. It underlined the role of the NHS in improving health, renewed an ideological commitment to equity in access and provision, and tackled the need to ensure quality through clinical governance and accountability to local communities. Of fundamental importance was the move to loosen the restrictions of the old tripartite structure (separating general practice, hospital and community health services) by moving towards unified budgets and imposing a duty of partnership. The major structural change introduced to deliver these policy goals was the formation of primary care groups (PCGs). As we have seen, that general practitioners would prove efficient as stewards of the NHS was largely an article of faith.

PCGs undertake three principal functions on behalf of their local populations:[9]

- to improve the health of the population and address health inequalities
- to develop primary and community health services
- to commission a range of community and hospital services.

They brought together local providers of primary and community services under a board representing local GPs, nurses, the local community, social services and the health authority. PCGs served populations averaging around 100,000 people and were expected to evolve over time, learning from existing arrangements and from their own experience (see Table 1.2).

Table 1.2: PCG levels

1. Supporting and advising the health authority in commissioning care for its population.
2. Taking devolved responsibility for managing the budget for health care as a sub-committee of the health authority.
3. Becoming established as a free-standing body accountable to the health authority for commissioning primary and secondary services.
4. Becoming established as a free-standing body accountable to the health authority for commissioning care, with added responsibility for the provision of community health services.

At levels one and two, PCGs operate as sub-committees of the health authority. At levels three and four they become independent primary care trusts (PCTs). For the initial period of operation, all PCGs would begin operating at either level one or level two. Following a period of consultation, shadow PCG boards were established in September 1998, preparatory to taking up their responsibilities. In April 1999, 481 PCGs were established throughout England. Seventeen of these formed the first wave of PCTs a year later; by April 2001, over one-third will have made this transition.

PCGs were saddled with heavy expectations. In obvious respects they represented an evolutionary advance as any attempt to 'universalise the best' of fundholding was bound to do. Their size, scope and key supports borrowed from their immediate precursors: total purchasing pilots and GP commissioning groups. Evaluation of total purchasing pilots suggested likely predictors of PCGs' 'success'. These included scale of investment in organisational development and support from the local health authority.[6] The experience of fundholding predicted possible concerns: for example, that PCGs serving healthier, wealthier areas might progress more swiftly to trust status than those serving needier populations. Nonetheless, the creation of budgets encompassing general medical services prescribing hospital and specialist care remained a major step forward. How have they fared?

Tracking progress

Work from the Audit Commission[10,11] and two recent evaluation reports funded by Department of Health[12,13] provide a comprehensive account of how PCGs are approaching their core functions. The broad conclusions are remarkably consistent. Establishing the organisation has been a key early preoccupation, and PCGs made sound progress in their first year. They have begun to translate priorities into clear local health strategies, targets and action plans. However, important challenges need to be addressed if PCG/Ts are to realise their undoubted potential.

Not all PCG boards function in a corporate manner, and there is a tendency for general practitioners to dominate board meetings at the expense of contributions from nurses, social services and lay members. There remain significant concerns about the degree to which practices are effectively engaged in the work of PCGs, and about the relative lack of progress in involving lay stakeholders.

Many health authorities and PCGs have struggled to find the right balance between 'letting go' and 'holding to account'. Health authorities retain an important role in strategic leadership via the health improvement programme (HImP) and co-ordination of the local health economy.[14] They have struggled to provide the support required for key areas of

PCGs' work. Management budgets have varied widely between PCGs, with clear consequences for their organisational development.

PCGs are getting to grips with their responsibilities for managing budgets, including the management of service level agreements and the development of incentive schemes, but many lack the necessary information and financial management capacity. A combination of unrealistic targets, a lack of resources, and the inadequacy of existing systems is seriously impeding PCGs' ability to generate the information needed for carrying out their core functions.

Many PCGs have made considerable progress in developing minimum standards for practice services, agreeing plans for redistributing resources and making service improvements. Most groups have made a good start in establishing an infrastructure for clinical governance and initiating a range of activities involving practices and other staff. Much more remains to be done, however, in finding ways of tackling poor performance and dealing with 'outliers'. In contrast, many PCGs have struggled to support commissioning or health improvement. Although most PCGs have begun to develop closer links with social services departments, relationships with the wider local authority are embryonic at this stage. Boundary differences remain an obstacle to closer partnership working.

There is a danger that national policy imperatives, central directives and guidance will stifle the development of local policies addressing local needs. PCGs testify to the demands of the PCT application process, and many wanted time to develop and deliver tangible changes for their practices before any such move. The decision to become a trust should be based not on administrative or financial considerations, or a desire for independence, but on a demonstration of how trust status will help deliver better services, combined with evidence of capacity to take on new roles and responsibilities. Finally, the traditional clinical focus on the individual patient needs to be counterbalanced by a stronger focus on population health. Medical models of health, illness and the role of health care need to be supplemented by wider definitions of health and support for the interventions necessary to address the social determinants of ill health.

In summary, PCGs are developing as organisations at different speeds. They have made progress in developing and integrating primary and community care, but their commissioning and health improvement functions as yet are limited. For many PCGs, much creative energy is being drained away in the process of application for trust status.

Personal medical services – the quieter revolution

Though initially eclipsed by PCGs, Labour eventually extended the personal medical services initiative. The PMS pilots proved unexpectedly popular after a slow start. The third wave of 1230 practices going live in April 2001 amounts to a fourfold increase. The Government expects as many as one-third of all GPs to be working under PMS the following year. They are preferentially distributed at this stage in urban, more deprived areas, where the salaried option has been heavily taken up. Some of the financial risks of running a practice are reduced and, unsurprisingly, a reduction in the bureaucratic burdens of the job is welcome to many GPs.[15] The salaried

GPs are happier with their income and hours of work than GMS GPs.[16]

But all has not been plain sailing. Some community trust-based pilots languished in the face of local medical committees' resistance to nurse-led primary care. Some community trusts underestimated the complexity of providing general medical services. In these instances, doctors found themselves taking on administrative responsibilities from which they had imagined they would be relieved. Defining measures of quality of primary care against which to hold practices to account is surprisingly difficult. An early content analysis found little evidence of more appropriate quality standards being incorporated into PMS contracts.[17] Much of what the first wave of pilots were seeking could have been achieved through the use of other red book flexibilities, and it is too early to state how much service development can properly be attributed to PMS. First wave pilots received an average of £62,893 extra on entering PMS, but there is as yet no hard evidence that they are delivering improvements in patient care in comparison with GMS practices.[16]

PMS provides entrepreneurs with some of the independence enjoyed by fundholders, but the pattern of expansion of PMS suggests that, in part, its success reflects its appeal to practices disaffected with the current reforms. Paradoxically, many practices see PMS as a way of defining their own priorities and insulating themselves from the intrusions of PCG/Ts. Unfortunately, such has been the pace of change that many PCG boards have lacked a strategic position on local PMS. They have certainly lacked the resources to provide developmental support. Nonetheless, PMS provides crucial leverage for the PCTs that will in future hold their contracts. For the first time, PCTs hold truly integrated budgets with the ability to commission local primary care. Where all practices are contracted to their local PCT, the vision of a UK-style health maintenance organisation is already being realised.

Addressing variations in quality

Variations in the quality of primary care, particularly in inner cities, have been a prominent concern of policy-makers since the inception of the NHS. The previous government sought to import organisation-wide quality improvement strategies perceived as successful in manufacturing and service industries. The 1989 White Paper *Working for patients* extolled the virtues of audit.[18] In some disciplines, 'the critical analysis of the quality of health care' was already established as best practice. What was new was an attempt to generalise audit activity. Over £500 million was spent on audit in the hospital and community sectors to mixed effect. The audit movement fell short of expectations in various ways.[19] First, audit topics reflected the priorities of doctors with little non-medical involvement (*cf.*, the shift from medical to clinical audit). Second, it proved difficult to routinise audit activity. *Working for patients* did not free resources for health professionals to dedicate time to audit. Finally, involvement remained patchy. Clinical audit did not engage the traditionally 'hard to reach'. Participation in audit was voluntary and not a contractual obligation upon general practitioners.

The invention of clinical governance heralded the latest of many attempts in the NHS to exercise greater managerial control over clinical activities. Governmental concerns over professional self-regulation were heightened in the wake of events at the Bristol Royal Infirmary and were about to be raised still more dramatically.

Table 1.3: The scope of clinical governance in primary care

- Clear lines of responsibility and accountability for the overall quality of clinical care.

- A comprehensive programme of quality improvement activities:

  (a) evidence-based practice
  (b) national service frameworks/NICE
  (c) workforce planning and development
  (d) continuing professional development
  (e) safeguarding patient confidentiality
  (f) clinical audit and outcomes
  (g) quality assurance
  (h) research and development.

- Risk management.

- Identification and remedy of poor performance.

Clinical governance has been defined as a system through which NHS organisations are accountable for continuously improving the quality of their services and safeguarding high standards of care by creating an environment in which clinical excellence will flourish.[20] It draws together elements of quality assurance that are often ill co-ordinated. The corporate nature of this new responsibility requires, in the overused phrase, major 'cultural change'. For PCG/Ts, this implies sharing intelligence about quality across professional and practice boundaries, and health professionals seeing themselves as collectively accountable for the clinical and cost effectiveness of their colleagues' work. Table 1.3 illustrates the scope of clinical governance in primary care.

Clinical governance presents particular challenges for PCGs. In setting their own clinical governance priorities they will have to reconcile national 'givens' with local concerns if the priorities they identify are to be 'owned' by their constituents. They need to link forward planning and implementation of clinical governance with primary care investment and the implementation of their local health improvement programme (HImP). Clinical governance implies a new understanding about the nature of professional accountability. Is there any evidence of progress where previous attempts to improve quality of care have failed?

Progress on clinical governance

The Audit Commission found wide differences between the amount that PCGs planned to spend on clinical governance in year one. This in turn ensured variable levels of local support in the form of new staff. Most PCGs appointed a doctor and nurse to share the brief.[11] Reporting mechanisms are in place and lines of accountability clarified, but the extent to which these have been internalised by clinical governance leads, let alone the 'rank and file', is more debatable. Many are scrambling up steep learning curves and only now are beginning to understand the complexity of their jobs.[21] Most PCGs have set up a clinical governance sub-committee. In over three-quarters of PCGs, practices have appointed their own clinical governance lead. However, levels of support from other agencies such as public health departments, academic bodies or education networks vary considerably.[21] While cross links with clinical governance structures and community trusts are developing swiftly, particularly among those planning an early transition to PCT status, links with the acute sector are largely invisible.

Clinical governance activity should be part of an integrated package focused on HImP priorities. Seven out of ten PCGs confirmed that their clinical governance programme would include inter-practice audit of treatment/referral for conditions mentioned in their HImP.[11] Most commonly these were heart disease, hypertension and diabetes. Improving data quality through the agreement of common coding classifications, for example, is a high priority, as is adverse event monitoring. However, only one in three PCGs are trying to agree evidence-based protocols for community or practice nursing interventions. It is important that clinical audit is not confined to medical issues and the treatment of specific conditions but examines the total package of care available to patient groups.

One enduring challenge is the search for a package of performance indicators to help identify sub-standard performance. The easily measurable is rarely useful. Technical obstacles, such as the difficulties of controlling for case-mix, are not easily resolved. Most indicators are influenced by factors outside the control of health systems. Measures of process will continue to be more useful than measures of outcome. The former can be truly 'evidence-based'.

The management of poor performance presents PCG/Ts with a major challenge. Complaints, colleagues' expressed concerns and financial audit visits by the health authority are the main means of detection at present. The consultation paper *Supporting doctors, protecting patients*[22] proposed compulsory annual audit and appraisal for all doctors, with assessment and support centres for failing doctors, but it is not yet clear how they will operate.

The emphasis has been on setting the right cultural tone as much as on concrete achievements. In the wake of the Shipman verdict, this has not been easy. PCG/Ts are trying to adopt a non-threatening, facilitative and developmental approach to clinical governance while setting up new local monitoring mechanisms.[23] The threats both to independent contractor status and professional self-regulation have increased doctors' feelings of beleaguerment. They are unconvinced by the rhetoric of a 'no blame' culture.

The access card

The New Labour administration was no less concerned than its predecessors to ensure timely access to care. The first National Patient Survey confirmed that difficulties booking appointments and waiting times for routine or emergency care were prominent public concerns.[24] Fair access formed one dimension of a new performance assessment framework but, at first sight, the raft of policy initiatives designed to improve access to primary care appeared populist and reflexive. Early commentaries on *The new NHS* White Paper concentrated on the structural reforms drawing attention away from NHS Direct, the national nurse-led telephone helpline. The purpose of the new service was to provide 'easier and faster advice and information for people about health, illness and the NHS so that they are better able to care for themselves and their families'. But NHS Direct was about more than a response to the consumerist demands of the 24-hour society. It followed the recommendations of the Chief Medical Officer's report

Developing emergency services in the community published earlier that year.[25] More specific objectives for NHS Direct included the encouragement of self-care at home and reducing unnecessary use of other NHS services, i.e. management of demand.[26]

The extension of NHS Direct on the basis of early research was oddly fumbled. The interim report of an evaluation funded by the NHSE hardly gave credence to claims that NHS Direct, though popular, was achieving its aims.[27] General practitioners were sceptical of claims that NHS Direct would reduce their workloads. They were quick to seize on the spinning of 'evidence' to rationalise a decision (on the extension of the service country-wide) already taken. The final report confirmed that the new service has had little impact on other emergency services.[28]

Already sensitive to threats to their professional monopoly over first contact care, the medical profession was therefore doubly wary of the introduction of walk-in centres. These were presented by Frank Dobson as a specific response to the apparent success of instant access primary care facilities established by the private sector, notably on railway stations serving time-pressed commuters. Anything Medicentres could provide, the NHS could provide better. More serious concerns revolved around the experience of walk-in centres in other countries, notably Canada.[29] Multiple access points with poorly co-ordinated record keeping could result in fragmented care. Most of the first wave of 36 were to be nurse-led. Walk-in centres were therefore easily conflated with other threats to the future of independent contractor status.

In summary, these innovations nicely crystallised the differences in priority different players attach to access. Their apparent popularity with patients contrasted with their reluctant acceptance by health professionals, but concerns over their cost effectiveness remain.

Modernising NHS dentistry

The balance of NHS and private dental care changed in the early 1990s. Discontent among dentists grew as their NHS fees were progressively reduced. In 1992/93, private work accounted for only five per cent of individual dentists' gross earnings; by 1996/97 this had gone up to 25 per cent.[30] The capacity of the NHS dental service as a whole has been reduced with predictable effects: 2 million people cannot gain access to NHS dentistry.

In the Autumn of 2000, the Government finally published its dental health strategy, and allocated around £160 million for its implementation over the next two years.[31] Almost all of the initiatives in the new strategy are aimed at the NHS general dental service. There will be a network of at least 50 walk-in dental access centres, each seeing some 10,000 patients each year. NHS Direct will provide advice on dental problems, nearest practices and dental access centres, out-of-hours services and the range of NHS treatments, including information on charges. In the dental surgery, patients will receive a full description of proposed treatment, with a clear distinction between NHS and private costs – an area in which many people have been confused.

There will also be positive changes affecting the work of NHS dentists. There will be loyalty payments of up to £4500 a year for older dentists working full-time in the NHS. A development fund will pay for extended premises or new equipment, and money will be available to improve the practices of 'significantly committed' NHS dentists. NHS dentists will start auditing the quality of their work and sharing it with colleagues, and will have to commit themselves to continuing professional development. The profession's self-regulation is to be strengthened.

It would be churlish, then, to dismiss the strategy, but overall it only partially addresses the problems of people who cannot access NHS dentistry.[32] Walk-in centres will help, but there will not be enough to solve the problem of access. These initiatives fail to tackle the main problem facing NHS dentistry: a shift of dental work into the private sector over the last eight years.

Community pharmacy

The organisation of high street pharmacy has traditionally been more influenced by market forces than by government policy.[33] Community pharmacy services have recently been undergoing significant changes. The proportion of pharmacist-owned pharmacies has dropped steadily. Forty per cent of pharmacists are now owned by pharmacy multiples with more than five outlets. There has been a sharp rise in the number of pharmacies located in superstores. With 6 million people visiting a pharmacist every day,[34] does this restructuring of pharmacies mean better access to services? The answer to this varies with the means of the user concerned. Superstores are accessible for those with cars but may be remote to those relying on failing public transport. A reduction of pharmacies in the high street is a cause for concern.

What of the role of the community pharmacist? The profession has long championed a vision of the pharmacist as the well-rounded clinician, offering far more than a simple dispensing service.[35] Yet, the in-coming Labour government proved reluctant to move quickly in this area. The pharmacy strategy – one of Frank Dobson's early promises – was only released in 2000.[36]

The new strategy confirmed a key role for community pharmacies in the implementation of *The NHS Plan* and the 'modernisation' of services. The respective roles of pharmacists and doctors are to be challenged. Pharmacists are to be given opportunities to take part in 'medicines management', responsible for their own case-load of patients with chronic disease. Access to services will be improved as more medicines are to be designated as pharmacy medicines, and dispensed by pharmacists without a doctor's prescription (although this may increase direct health care costs met by patients themselves). The most obvious example of this change has been that of emergency hormonal contraception (the 'morning after pill') which has been deregulated, albeit controversially. Electronic prescribing – an obvious symbol of 'modernisation' – will be introduced to reduce the time it takes patients to receive their medicines.

In line with dentistry and general practice, the Government has introduced local contracting for services. New pilots of local pharmacy services will replace the national contractual arrangements and, arguably, reduce the capacity for collective bargaining by the profession's representatives. Interestingly, the Government seems less hesitant in promoting competition between professionals in relation to pharmacy than it does with regard to other professions. The control over market entry that has for so long restricted the opening of new pharmacies may be abandoned in some areas in favour of open competition. Finally, the theme of service integration features strongly. Pharmacy advice will soon form part of NHS Direct and one-stop primary care centres will incorporate pharmacists into a wide range of local services.

New Labour, new crises ... new Plan

Recent reforms of the NHS have owed as much to the reactions of prime ministers to perceived crises of public confidence as to premeditated planning within the Department of Health. As with Margaret Thatcher's impulsive decision to instigate market-oriented changes in 1988,[1] Tony Blair appeared to take the rest of his government by surprise when he announced ambitious new spending plans early in 2000. These were to raise health expenditure to the European average within five years and were an implicit acknowledgement that his mission to modernise the NHS was foundering. Public failures – particularly those of the medical profession – armed the Government to challenge entrenched medical interests and strengthened the case for reform.

As well as amounting to their next election manifesto, *The NHS Plan* that emerged six months later represents a 'new deal' between the Government and the health sector[37] (Table 1.4). In return for substantial new funding, the Government seeks to challenge some of the long-established foundations of the NHS and, in particular, to revisit the settlement between organised medicine and the State. The Plan itself is a curious mix of the profound and the mundane – from an ambitious public health agenda to televisions at every hospital bedside. It provides a litany of new investments and targets for service improvement, and has been broadly welcomed by medical and nursing interest groups.

Table 1.4: *The NHS Plan* – Key points

> ◆ 2000 more GPs and 450 more registrars by 2004
> ◆ 500 one-stop health centres by 2004
> ◆ 3000 surgeries upgraded by 2004
> ◆ NHS Lift, a new private–public partnership to develop premises
> ◆ 1000 specialist GPs
> ◆ Consultants delivering 4 million out-patient appointments in primary care
> ◆ 2100 extra acute and general hospital beds
> ◆ 5000 extra intermediate care beds
> ◆ Out-patient appointments to drop from six to three months
> ◆ Patients given copies of clinicians' letters
> ◆ Single-handed GPs to sign up to 'new contractual quality standards'
> ◆ Annual appraisals next year
> ◆ Mandatory audit from next year to support revalidation
> ◆ The GMC to be part of new umbrella organisation of regulatory bodies
> ◆ Assessment centres to oversee doctors' performance from 2001

The Plan represents incrementalism rather than a radical change in government policy. Alternative methods of funding health care (private insurance, co-payments, social insurance) were explicitly rejected. The Plan confirms the direction set out in the Labour government's first policy statement,[8] and key policy themes are reaffirmed. These include:

(a) *Investment in infrastructure and workforce* – The Plan

signals a major investment in new staff and facilities. The NHS workforce is set to increase with 7000 more consultants, 2000 more GPs, 20,000 more nurses and 6500 more therapists all promised. For the first time in many years, a government has committed itself to increase the number of hospital beds. £1 billion is to be invested in practice premises. However, the Plan also seeks to reshape service delivery through additional capital development. New 'diagnostic and treatment centres' will be developed over four years, delivering day care and short stay treatment in an effort to separate elective and emergency facilities and speed the reduction of waiting lists. Intermediate care receives £900m.

(b) Increased access to health services – New targets guarantee access to a primary care professional within 24 hours and to a general practitioner within 48 hours. NHS Direct and walk-in centres are to be extended nationwide, despite limited evidence as yet that they relieve demand elsewhere in the system.[28]

(c) Demand management – NHS Direct will nevertheless provide access to a number of different primary care providers, nurse-led and, theoretically, more cost efficient. The same substitution of less expensive human resources is reflected in new extended roles for pharmacists. Ten key roles for nurses equip them to take on hitherto medical tasks in line with their North American counterparts. GP sub-specialists similarly will take on work previously undertaken by hospital consultants.

(d) Integration of health and social services – Though they are only slowly developing their purchasing functions, PCTs provide a vehicle for the increasing integration of health and social care. New PCTs bring health and social services into

one organisation, and managerial responsibility will be unified under a single chief executive. These structures are unlikely to overcome all the long-standing barriers to joint working at this interface, but this remains a logical progression.

(e) Partnership for health improvement – This government's commitment to addressing health inequalities has always distinguished it from its predecessor. The Plan sets challenging targets for disease reduction, building on the earlier national health strategy.[38] These include the reduction of cancer deaths in under-75s by 20 per cent. A commitment to health promotion is reflected in proposals for a new national screening programme for colo-rectal cancer, money to back smoking cessation strategies, and a pledge to distribute free fruit as part of a new campaign to improve children's diets. The role of the new primary care organisations in delivering public health remains ill-defined.

(f) User empowerment – A series of developments are supposed to bring patients and citizens into decision-making at every level of the service. Patients are to receive more information, for example about their practice (size, accessibility, performance against national standards – the much feared 'league tables'). A new patient advocacy and liaison service in hospitals and increasing scrutiny over the NHS by local authorities spell the end for existing community health councils (CHCs). These changes form just one part of the drive to increase professional accountability.

(g) The public–private concordat – Labour has made much of new constructive links with the private sector, playing down their traditionally oppositional relationship. Public funds may support private provision when necessary, for example in

reducing waiting times. The private finance initiative – opposed vehemently by Labour in opposition – is to be extended in support of the new hospital building programme and practice premises development.

(h) Increasing accountability – The Government feel they have fulfilled their part of the bargain but will expect more than just 'principled motivation' in return. The early emphasis by the Labour government on increased regulation of professionals is considerably strengthened under the Plan. The most significant change to the ways GPs work will be the elaboration by 2004 of a new contractual framework, building on the stipulations for improved outcomes that are supposed to be inherent in the PMS approach. Single-handed practices are an immediate focus for this.

(i) Performance management – New Labour has been repeatedly criticised for its centralising tendencies at the expense of local experimentation. Henceforth, subject to satisfactory performance, NHS bodies are promised considerable freedom from central supervision and interference ('earned autonomy'), but new accountability structures are being created. A modernisation agency will oversee implementation of the Plan and will advise the Secretary of State. Specific task-forces in at least 12 clinical or managerial areas are being created 'to drive forward implementation'. Trying to trace the interconnections between these new organisations will be a bewildering entertainment in itself. A system of 'earned autonomy' implies robust systems for measuring progress. PCG/Ts will be required to meet well-defined criteria to access the National Performance Fund. The next version of the performance assessment framework

embracing PCTs is awaited with interest; its predecessors have been underwhelming.

Conclusion

The out-going Conservative government presented the new Labour administration with many of the tools it has wielded in its quest for modernisation. The internal market has been adapted in gradualist fashion within a framework of mandatory collective funding. In other respects this government's first four years have proved unexpectedly radical. Least clearly foreseen was the series of initiatives designed to change the nature of first contact and to free up access to health care. It is to these that we now turn.

References

[1] NHS Executive. *Developing NHS purchasing and GP fundholding: towards a primary care-led NHS.* (EL(94)79) London: HMSO, 1994.

[2] Audit Commission. *What the doctor ordered: a study of GP fundholding in England and Wales.* London: HMSO, 1996.

[3] Mays N, Goodwin N, Killoran A, Malbon G, on behalf of the Total Purchasing National Evaluation Team. *Total purchasing: a step towards primary care groups.* London: King's Fund, 1999.

[4] Le Grand J, Mays N, Mulligan J, editors. *Learning from the NHS internal market. A review of the evidence.* London: King's Fund, 1998.

[5] Secretaries of State for Health in England, Wales and Scotland. *Choice and opportunity. Primary care: the future.* London: HMSO, 1996.

[6] Lewis R, Gillam S, editors. *Transforming primary care. Personal medical services in the new NHS.* London: King's Fund, 1999.

[7] Department of Health. *The NHS (Primary Care) Act 1997.* London: The Stationery Office, 1997.

[8] Department of Health. *The new NHS: modern, dependable.* London: The Stationery Office, 1997.

[9] Department of Health. *The new NHS Modern and*

dependable: primary care groups: delivering the agenda. HSC 1998/228. Leeds: Department of Health, 1998.

[10] Audit Commission. *PCGs: an early view of primary care groups in England.* London: Audit Commission, 1999.

[11] Audit Commission. *The PCG agenda: early progress of primary care groups in 'The new NHS'.* London: Audit Commission, 2000.

[12] Smith J, Regen E, Goodwin N *et al. Getting into their stride. Interim report of a national evaluation of primary care groups.* Birmingham: University of Birmingham, Health Services Management Centre, 2000.

[13] Wilkin D, Gillam S, Leese B, editors. *The national tracker survey of primary care groups and trusts. Progress and challenges 1999/2000.* London: National Primary Care Research and Development Centre/King's Fund, 2000.

[14] NHS Executive. *Leadership for health: the health authority role.* Leeds: NHS Executive, 1999.

[15] Huntington J, Walsh N, Barnes M, Rogers R, Baines D. This is your pilot speaking. *Health Services Journal* 2000; 3 Aug: 30–31.

[16] The National PMS Evaluation Team. *National evaluation of first wave NHS personal medical services pilots: integrated interim report from four research projects.* Manchester: National Primary Care Research and Development Centre, 2000.

[17] Lewis R, Gillam S, Gosden T, Sheaff R. Who contracts for primary care? *Journal of Public Health Medicine* 1999; 21: 367–71.

[18] Secretary of State for Health. *Working for patients.* London: HMSO, CM 555.78, 1989.

[19] Spencer J. Audit in general practice: where do we go from here? *Quality in Health Care* 1993; 2: 183–88.

[20] NHS Executive. *A first class service: quality in the new NHS.* London: Department of Health, 1998.

[21] Hayward J, Rosen R, Dewar S. Thin on the ground. *Health Services Journal* 1999; 26 Aug: 6–27.

[22] NHS Executive. *Supporting doctors, protecting patients.* London: The Stationery Office, 1999.

[23] Wye L, Rosen R, Dewar S. *Clinical governance in primary care. A review of baseline assessments.* London: King's Fund, 2000.

[24] NHS Executive. *The national surveys of NHS patients. General practice 1998.* London: Department of Health, 1999.

[25] Calman K. *Developing emergency services in the community. The final report.* London: NHS Executive, 1997.

[26] Rosen R, Florin D. Evaluating NHS Direct. *BMJ* 1999; 319: 5–6.

[27] Munro J, Nicholl J, O'Cathain A, Knowles E. *Evaluation of NHS Direct first wave sites. First interim report to the Department of Health.* Sheffield: Medical Care Research Unit, University of Sheffield, 1998.

[28] Munro J, Nicholl J, O'Cathain A, Knowles E. *Evaluation of NHS Direct first wave sites. Second interim report to the Department of Health.* Sheffield: Medical Care Research Unit, University of Sheffield, 2000.

[29] Jones M. Walk-in primary care centres: lessons from Canada. *BMJ* 2000; 321: 928–31.

[30] Hayward J. NHS dentistry. In: *Health Care UK 1999/2000.* London: King's Fund: 98–107.

[31] NHS Executive. *Modernising dentistry.* London: NHSE, 2000.

[32] Keen J, Hayward J. (Personal communication).

[33] Lewis, R. The future of community pharmacy. *The Guardian* 2001, 17 January.

[34] Secretary of State for Health. *Primary care: the future.* Leeds: NHS Executive, 1996.

[35] Royal Pharmaceutical Society of Great Britain. *Building the future – a strategy for a 21st century pharmaceutical service.* London: RPSGB, 1997.

[36] NHS Executive. *Pharmacy strategy.* London: NHSE, 2000.

[37] NHS Executive. *The NHS Plan. A plan for investment. A plan for reform.* Cm 4818-I. London: The Stationery Office, 2000.

[38] NHS Executive. *Saving lives: our healthier nation.* Leeds: NHSE, 1998.

Chapter 2: Improving access to primary care

Dominique Florin

Introduction

Improving access to primary health care has been a recurrent theme of the Government's modernisation programme. Initiatives include new services such as NHS Direct and walk-in centres, as well as a commitment in *The NHS Plan* for the NHS to reduce waiting times for GP appointments to a maximum of 48 hours.[1]

This government is not the first to grapple with the problem of poor access to primary care and, in part, this is evidence of the perceived vote-winning potential of this issue. The 1990 reforms to the GP contract included measures designed to improve access to GPs, such as linking pay to their hours of availability.[2] Access and availability are aspects of health care that patients particularly value.[3] In international terms, the NHS has been characterised as having a 'waiting list culture', and while waiting lists are not unique to the UK, neither are they universal. Other countries have designed systems with improved access but these may have significant costs.

Improving access involves increasing capacity and/or flexibility.[4] This often implies trade-offs with other aspects of quality. For example, an older patient with a chronic disease may particularly value access to a known GP, and be able and willing to attend the surgery during normal working hours. Conversely, a younger working patient may be satisfied with a more 'anonymous' contact, whether in person or over the phone, at a convenient time.

In this chapter, different components of access are explored, both to understand how access relates to other aspects of quality in primary care and to analyse the implications for access of current developments such as NHS Direct, the increasing role of nurses and walk-in centres. Will these innovations increase access and decrease inequalities in primary care without compromising other aspects of quality?

What do we mean by access in primary care?

From the recent policy pronouncements on access in primary care, it is possible to interpret the dominant construction of access as being mainly concerned with convenience and reassurance of the 'worried well'. There is a risk that other important meanings of access are not being addressed (particularly concerning inequalities) and there are costs of focusing on this particular understanding of access.

Access to health care encompasses several dimensions: access to different health professionals, in person or in other ways, for advice or treatment, urgently or routinely. The Royal College of General Practitioners (RCGP) has compiled a description of access in primary care.[5] They suggest that most patients access the NHS through general practice consultations on the telephone, in the surgery or at home, and may involve contact with GPs, practice nurses, or other members of the primary health care team. In addition, there are contacts with a variety of out-of-hours arrangements. Other methods of access include advice by pharmacists or through NHS Direct, walk-in centres, community nursing, accident and emergency, genito-urinary medicine clinics and mental health emergency clinics. The RCGP suggests that general practice provides not only the commonest route of access but also the preferred route: a personal consultation in the context of a long-term relationship and the life-long record. In reality, other facilities are more commonly used – such as pharmacists with whom 6 million people interact each day[6] – but the RCGP vision of general practice and primary care is closely linked with modes of access that preserve the primacy and centrality of the GP role.

The table below illustrates some of the dimensions of access. There are key links with equity and with continuity of care, and with capacity in primary care and its ability to reconcile supply and demand factors. This typology also brings out aspects of access such as convenience, possible differences between professional and lay concepts of appropriateness, the issue of flexibility and the interchangeability of roles (between doctors and nurses in particular), and the gate-keeping role of GPs.

Table 2.1: Dimensions of access

For whom?	Well or ill users, hard to reach groups, ethnic minorities, special needs
For what?	Information, advice, reassurance, treatment
When?	In- and out-of-hours, for routine or emergency care
To whom?	Different health professionals
To what?	Primary or secondary care, different sectors
How?	Telephone, Internet, face to face, in a surgery or at home

The wide scope of access to and through primary care suggests that a single 'gateway' may not to be able to cover the full range of modalities or groups requiring access. Conversely, increasing the number of gateways will only improve access if they enter the same space.

Access as a dimension of quality in primary care

The quality of primary care is comprised of timely access to high quality clinical and interpersonal care.[3] The aspects of general practice most valued by patients are availability and access (both appointments and telephone access), technical competence, communication skills, interpersonal attributes and the organisation of care (including continuity). Within this constellation of attributes, Hodgkin has suggested that 'patients typically rate continuity of care way below communication, competence and accessibility',[7] but more research is needed to disentangle patient preferences and to understand the possible trade-offs involved. Increasing access may have an effect on the other dimensions, especially continuity of care. There is some evidence that continuity is associated with increased patient satisfaction and positive health outcomes, lower costs and lower referral rates.[8] Improving access will not inevitably lower the quality of primary care in other respects but, in assessing the impact of initiatives on access, we need to weigh up different outcomes such as convenience, equity, continuity, costs and effectiveness.

Initiatives increasing access: the balance sheet

In the remainder of this chapter, four areas of development will be examined: NHS Direct, walk-in centres, out-of-hours care and changes in professional roles.

NHS Direct

Origins

NHS Direct has been for this government an important symbol of its modernism and responsiveness. This nurse telephone advice line was launched in three trial sites in March 1998 and is now being rolled out nationally. NHS Direct was conceived of following a review of emergency services in 1997.[9] The stated aims of the service are to provide 24-hour health advice, to encourage self-care and to reduce demands on other NHS services.[10] In documents directed at the public, convenience and the reduction of anxiety are emphasised: 'NHS Direct, the confidential telephone advice line staffed by nurses, open 24 hours a day, every day ... NHS Direct aims to give you: Guidance on what to do when you have a health worry. What might this niggling pain be? Should I call the doctor?'[11]

NHS Direct has been a source of considerable controversy amongst GPs. There is tension between a consumerist view that there cannot be too much access and that 24-hour availability is always 'a good thing', and a professional view that increasing supply may increase demand independently of need, that is, create 'inappropriate' demands, for instance for medical reassurance in the face of minor self-limiting problems. Can lay (or political) as opposed to professional definitions of appropriateness be reconciled?

Impact

Interim evaluations show a largely out-of-hours advice service that is growing in popularity receives high satisfaction ratings and seems to be safe.[10,12,13] It has proved more difficult to demonstrate either an increase or a decrease in self-care and self-reliance, or an impact on the use of other services. The latest evaluation has not detected any impact on use of A&E or rates of ambulance calls, but did find an association, which may or may not be causal, with a halting in the upward rise in use of GP co-operatives. The evaluations have not answered a number of other important questions, such as effects of the service on equity or continuity.

Several groups are disadvantaged in respect of access to health care. Initially, NHS Direct was offered only in English, but it is now being developed in a way that may make it more accessible to those whose first language is not English. For NHS Direct it is essential to ensure that factors such as age, disability, ethnicity, language and cultural differences do not limit access. At present, NHS Direct is used mainly as an out-of-hours service, yet groups with relatively higher use of GP out-of-hours services,[14] older people and those from some ethnic minorities are currently those least likely to use it.[10]

While some NHS Direct sites are linked to GP co-operatives, others are not. This is unfortunate, as the development of out-of-hours GP co-operatives has demonstrated the strengths of GPs voluntarily working together across practices in order to address a long-standing problem in access. This also touches on the issue of continuity of care, which is likely to be decreased if NHS Direct functions as a stand-alone service.

The future
Equivocal results concerning the effectiveness or cost effectiveness of the service are unlikely to halt the further development of NHS Direct. NHS Direct has now been rolled out nationally and its functions are set to expand. Integration of NHS Direct with other local services and attempts to improve

access for disadvantaged groups may address concerns over continuity of care and equity. The Department of Health now suggests that NHS Direct should become the single point of access for all out-of-hours contacts[15] – even the gateway for all NHS contacts at any time of day or night.[5,16] The greater use of telephone triage is appealing, but there are significant doubts as to the capacity of the service to cope with the much increased activity that this would entail, especially given shortages of nurses.[17] With further expansion, local focus may prove even more difficult to maintain. The potential for bureaucratic confusion will be understood by anyone who has tried to connect with other government services through a single national phone number.

Walk-in centres

In April 1999, the Prime Minister announced the introduction of 36 NHS walk-in centres intended to 'improve access to and convenience of primary care services', at an initial cost of £31 million.[18] These centres have a historical antecedent in private walk-in clinics such as the Medicentre chain, which have been a questionable success financially. Walk-in centres are being set up in response to perceived access problems to general practice, but they are not intended to replace or threaten general practice, rather to complement it. Responses have been divided, reflecting both an element of professional territorialism but also uncertainty as to the wider repercussions of the new service.

In a sense, walk-in centres are an extension of NHS Direct, in that they provide a nurse-led open-access service that to some extent occupies the same territory as traditional general practice. The major rationale for walk-in centres is convenience, particularly for workers. This is reflected in the extension of opening beyond normal working hours and their siting in places such as airports and shopping centres. In the Department of Health's words, walk-in centres 'are being introduced to help anyone whose modern, busy lifestyle, or practical circumstances and particular needs, make flexible and accessible services so important'.[19] A further function is that of triage, similar to NHS Direct. There is also an interest in equity, with some centres sited in areas poorly served by primary care. The encouragement for the sites to be physically located next to other NHS facilities such as A&E departments or GP surgeries suggests a concern with integration and continuity of care with established services, although it as yet unclear how this will work in practice. Certainly the centres are expected to communicate details of patients' attendance (assuming consent) to the usual doctor. The converse, of course, is not the case, and consultations take place without access to patients' medical histories. This is contrary to a key principle of traditional general practice, but it remains to be seen whether the outcomes of consultations will be significantly the worse for it.

Walk-in centres are at an early stage in their development, with individual clinics just opening. A national evaluation has begun. However, it is noticeable that in contrast to NHS Direct, the aims of the service have not been made so explicit in policy statements – for instance in terms of expected impact on other services or in terms of increasing self-care. Most descriptions of the anticipated service have stressed process aspects, such as convenient siting and opening hours. The evaluation will look at quality of care, effectiveness and appropriateness, but it will be difficult to demonstrate walk-in centres' impact on local health economies, given their relatively small scale.

At present, the impact of walk-in centres in the UK is unknown. There are similar theoretical dangers to those discussed in relation to NHS Direct, perhaps more so in relation to continuity of care. The relatively small scale of walk-in centres seems unlikely to ameliorate the access problems in general practice, and there is a possibility that patients may choose to use walk-in centres repeatedly and possibly 'inappropriately'. As already mentioned, professional constructions of appropriateness do not readily tally with lay understandings. Anecdotal accounts from some walk-in centres which have already opened suggest that repeat attendees with problems that would be better dealt with in a general practice are a problem,[20] whereas other users may have self-limiting complaints that do not require medical or nursing input. If they remain small scale, it is unlikely that they will have much impact on demand for general practice or pose any threat to the 'GP role'. However, if the new service becomes sizeable, the issue of complementarity with GP services becomes much more important. In that case, far greater integration between general practice and a nurse-led walk-in service will be necessary to avoid fragmentation of services and care.

There are some lessons to be learnt from the international experience, particularly in Canada,[21,22] where walk-in centres developed from the late-1970s onwards. The centres represent about three per cent of total first contact health expenditure and deal mainly with minor ailments. They are cheaper than A&E care but similar in cost to general practice. Because they are doctor-led (unlike UK walk-in centres), there is debate as to their appropriate role *vis-à-vis* general practice. Their lack of integration with other services is evidenced by a lack of continuity of care between the centres and general practices. Overall, there is little evidence for their effectiveness or economic impact.

Out-of-hours care

Although the problems with access to primary care are not solely out-of-hours, this aspect has taken on particular prominence. It is notable that NHS Direct has been used principally as an out-of-hours service.[10] In some cases the GP services provided out-of-hours are not well known or easily accessible, leading people to prefer NHS Direct. Evidently, the distinction between in-hours and out-of-hours is eroded in many areas of modern life and this is also the case in the context of health care. Out-of-hours care will increasingly no longer be solely about emergencies but will incorporate more routine types of health care.[23]

A major development in out-of-hours care over the last few years has been the advent of GP co-operatives. Different pressures resulted in the traditional model of out-of-hours care being revised. GPs have become reluctant to be personally on call for patients throughout the night, especially given the increase in out-of-hours calls over the last decades.[24] There were also concerns regarding the quality of care provided by deputising services (the 1990 contract introduced financial incentives to reduce their use) and the rise in attendances at A&E departments. Different approaches to out-of-hours were facilitated with the establishment in 1995 of a £45 million fund for out-of-hours developments and reformation of the associated fee structure. Between 1993 and 1997 membership of the National Association of GP Co-operatives increased from 31 to 261.[25]

One of the most notable features of out-of-hour co-operatives has been the extent to which they have been initiated and led by GPs themselves. A national evaluation of out-of hour co-operatives revealed that they have much improved members' quality of life and frequently provide a forum for educational activities.[25] However, other findings are less positive. There has been a rise in demand on the co-operatives, financial constraints have limited some developments, there are concerns regarding the quality and lack of continuity of care, and co-operatives have tended to be uni-professional. Patients generally prefer home visits to telephone advice,[26] but seem equally satisfied with deputising, practice-based and co-operative services.[27]

The recent review of out-of-hours care by the Department of Health[15] contains important suggestions for a much more highly planned and managed service. These include the proposal to make NHS Direct the first point of contact for all calls by 2004, explicit and monitored quality standards for all out-of-hours provision, improved integration between providers, and an administrative role for PCG/Ts. Once again, these suggestions have raised fears about the loss of the 'traditional' general practice role and the continuity of relationships both within and out-of-hours.[28]

A New Labour construction is that out-of-hours care is about care at convenient times, but research confirms an important equity aspect. Both the National Patient Survey and other work have shown that traditionally disadvantaged groups – those from deprived areas, the elderly and those from ethnic minorities – are more likely to use out-of-hours care.[14,29] The reasons for this are not fully understood but may reflect difficulty in accessing care in 'normal' hours. Furthermore, some areas of clinical care routinely require care out-of-hours, such as palliative care or mental health.[30,31] Disentangling these different access needs is complicated. Making NHS Direct the single triage point out-of-hours may be one solution, but better access to care within hours is also required.

Changes in professional roles

Integral to many attempts to improve access has been the eliding and expansion of roles of members of the primary health care team, particularly doctors and nurses. We have seen the development of nurse practitioners, nurse triage, nurses taking on traditional medical roles, and GPs and nurses taking on management functions and complex chronic disease care. *The NHS Plan* has restated the trend for expanded nurse roles, particularly into prescribing.[1] *The NHS Plan* also suggests expansion of the pharmacist role, specifically as a way of reducing demand on GP surgeries, for example by taking on the responsibility for repeat prescribing. These changes in the nature of the primary health care team are not only about improving access and managing demand within primary care, but also reflect other trends, such as the development of intermediate care, the shift of care from the secondary to the primary sector (and thus GPs taking on consultant roles) and the expansion of primary care-based commissioning.

These trends pre-date New Labour, but the advent of NHS Direct and walk-in centres has renewed the expansion of nurse roles into territory previously occupied by doctors, such as diagnosis. With respect to improving access, the aim of the expansion of nurse roles has been to increase flexibility without necessarily increasing staff capacity. In international terms, the UK is relatively 'under doctored', so it seems to make sense to re-allocate some medical roles to nursing colleagues. However, there are also currently 17,000 nurse vacancies in a NHS workforce of 300,000. How can initiatives that require increases in nurses do other than take nurses away from other areas of health care? *The NHS Plan* promises an increase of 20,000 nurses by 2004, but the significance of this figure has recently been disputed by the Royal College of Nurses since it does not refer to whole-time equivalents. Nevertheless, nurses taking on new roles present an opportunity both for professional development and for improved demand management and patient care.[1] Research into telephone and face-to-face nurse consultations has suggested that these are as safe as doctor consultations and cost no more.[10,12,32] Patient satisfaction with face-to-face nurse consultations seems to be at least as high as for doctor consultations, assuming that patients are given a choice of consulting either a doctor or a nurse.[32]

Prospects

New Labour's attempts to increase access are changing the shape of local health economies and the ways in which patients relate to their health services. We do not yet know the impact of many of these changes. The initiatives described above may increase access to primary care but also pose problems for a traditional model of primary care. Their impact on the overall quality of primary care or in economic terms is not clear. There is potential for a more integrated and responsive service, but the tensions described in this chapter need to be made explicit as part of an open debate between users, professionals and policy-makers.

Supply factors

On the whole, the solutions above do not directly address inadequate supply, and this is probably a significant contributor to delays in access in the UK. *The NHS Plan* pledges increases in the numbers of general practitioners and nurses. However, the actual increases may not be as much as initially appeared or indeed sufficient to meet commitments, such as access for patients to a GP within 48 hours. It is not clear whether they will compensate for the high retirement rates that are imminent in some parts of the country. One option that has apparently not been considered by policy-makers would be to reduce list size and provide longer consultations. This could improve quality, but improving both quality and access by reducing list sizes would require still larger increases in numbers (and expenditure).

Inequalities in access to primary care

Concern with inequalities of access is not the prime mover for developments such as NHS Direct, walk-in centres or other access initiatives. The impact of these new developments on inequalities needs to be specifically addressed and monitored. The National Patient Survey[14] shows that certain groups have systematically more difficulty in accessing primary care than others. More broadly, there is strong evidence that the distribution of primary care resources across England is inequitable, with poorer resources in more deprived areas such as the north and in inner cities.[34] Ultimately, attempts to improve access must address these structural problems. If they do not, existing inequalities will be reinforced, even if other aspects, such as convenience, improve for some groups.

Integration

There is a need to generate solutions within existing models, building on the known strengths of UK general practice.[35] One failure of some access initiatives has been the relative lack of integration with existing services. Ideally, access should improve by adjusting the existing system rather than by duplicating services. Likewise, there is a need to develop policy solutions in a medico-politically sensitive way. Unfortunately, the introduction of NHS Direct was not preceded by sufficient discussion to fuse professional and political views as to its purpose. As a result, NHS Direct was introduced in a way that cut across existing primary care structures. This meant that NHS Direct was seen by some GPs as cosmetic populism. More fundamentally, it was a failure of 'joined-up' policy-making that did not take into account the range of ways of resolving problems of access in primary care.

A potentially useful way of increasing access in an integrated way is through telephone triage – but within existing structures such as GP practices rather than in add-on structures such as NHS Direct. There is undoubtedly potential for phone consultations to increase patients' access to their own GPs and primary health care teams. Compared to the USA, this is an under-used option in UK general practice. The concept of triage is also important. There is scope for further research into the acceptability of telephone triage and consultation, and ways of improving this. The lower levels of satisfaction with telephone advice by out-of-hours services in contrast to NHS Direct may relate to differences in patient expectations.

Perhaps users who phone NHS Direct have no expectation of face-to-face contact, unlike those contacting GP-run services. One lesson from the USA – potentially applicable to an expanded role for NHS Direct – is that where triage is perceived as a barrier to access, it is highly unacceptable to users.[36]

Appropriateness and self-care

New Labour is keen to promote self-care, but there is little evidence as to how to do so. In one sense, phoning a NHS-funded helpline or consulting a nurse at a walk-in centre is no more self-care than consulting a GP. There is also little evidence so far on the cost effectiveness of different options. There have been claims from the profession that increased access will decrease self-care and increase dependency and demand, but little evidence exists for this. Nevertheless, it is reasonable to question whether there can be too much access. The interrelations of need, demand and supply may mean that increased access for some means less choice for others.

Hutchison has suggested that public education interventions may be a better way to promote self-care than walk-in clinics.[22] Communicating distinctions about appropriate use of care to patients is difficult, as attested by the numbers of attendances in general practice for minor, self-limiting problems. The choice to attend for a consultation with a health professional, in whatever setting, is a complex one and not always related to the severity or chronicity of the presenting complaint. In a similar debate over 'inappropriate' use of A&E departments in the 1980s and 1990s, it became clear that the service itself had to alter in order to meet users' needs – rather than trying to educate users to use primary care instead of the

A&E service in certain circumstances.[23] As a result, primary care doctors were sited within A&E departments, and most evidence seems to suggest better use of resources as a consequence.

Continuity

NHS Direct has been construed as posing a threat to the continuity of primary care services. Despite a lack of conclusive evidence, there is an intuitive argument that in moving from a registered list system, as in general practice, to more plural provision, continuity will be lost. However, increasingly modern general practice acknowledges a concept of continuity that does not centre on the relationship between a particular health professional and patient, but is linked to a whole team of professionals and to continuity of access to health records.[8] Locally, NHS Direct may be organised to dovetail into such systems. It has been claimed that certain patient groups, for example younger working people, do not value continuity. There is insufficient robust evidence to support this view, but for some forms of primary care contact, continuity may simply not be important – such as for minor illness events with no sequelae. There are also other open access services – such as A&E – that carry the same risks to continuity of primary care, but for which the benefits are thought to outweigh the disadvantages of possible loss of continuity. For example, the public health benefits of a separate, confidential service for sexually transmitted diseases outweigh the potential costs of lack of continuity with other primary care services.

Salisbury has suggested that several developments in primary care may undermine continuity of care, and that it is up to the public and the profession to decide just how important an aspect of primary care continuity is, and to design services accordingly.[30] The same logic applies to convenience. By focusing on convenience of access we may be missing other more important aspects of users' experience of health care.

Conclusion: who holds the gate?

By increasing both the multiplicity of access points to the NHS and the range of professionals at those points, the primacy of the GP as 'gate-keeper' is reduced. The gate-keeping – or gate-opening – role is one of the core features of UK general practice and is seen as one of the main ways of controlling costs in the system.[35] Successful gate-keeping depends on a number of factors: patients registered with a single GP or practice, a lack of alternative routes into secondary care, GPs who are willing to take on implicit responsibility for rationing, and patients who accept the restriction of access to secondary care except through their own GP. The last two imply a social contract between GPs and patients requiring high levels of trust and knowledge between parties. Evidently, nurses and other health professionals can be, indeed are, gate-keepers. Difficulties may arise, however, if there are multiple points of entry into secondary care, if poor knowledge of the patient makes it difficult to decide whether secondary care referral is appropriate, or if the context of the contact is anonymous rather than part of continuing care. In these circumstances, an important element of cost control in the UK system will be lost. Patient satisfaction will decline if triage and the new gate-keepers are still perceived as limiting access and thus controlling costs in the new NHS.[36]

References

[1] Secretary of State for Health. *The NHS Plan.* London: The Stationery Office, 2000.

[2] Department of Health. Health Departments of Great Britain. *General practice in the National Health Service: the 1990 contract.* London: HMSO, 1989.

[3] Roland M. Quality and efficiency: enemies or partners? *British Journal of General Practice* 1999; 49: 140–43.

[4] Murray M. Modernising the NHS. Patient care: access. *BMJ* 2000; 320: 1594–96.

[5] Royal College of General Practitioners. *Access to the NHS. Proposals for changes to the delivery of health services in England. A contribution to the 'modernisation' review.* Position statement no. 3, 2000. http://www.rcgp.org.uk/rcgp/corporate/position/modernisation

[6] Department of Health. *Primary care: delivering the future.* London: HMSO, 1996a.

[7] Hodgkin P, Logan A. Postcards from a new century. The hollow man – have GPs abandoned their core role? *British Journal of General Practice* 2000; 50: 516–17.

[8] Guthrie B, Wyke S. Controversy in primary care. Does continuity in general practice really matter? *BMJ* 2000; 321: 734–36.

[9] Calman K. *Developing emergency services in the community.*

The final report. London: NHS Executive, 1997.

[10] Munro J, Nicholl J, O'Cathain A, Knowles E. *Evaluation of NHS Direct first wave sites. First interim report to the Department of Health.* Sheffield: Medical Care Research Unit, School of Health and Related Research, University of Sheffield, 1998.

[11] http://www.nhsdirect.nhs.uk

[12] Munro J, Nicholl J, O'Cathain A, Knowles E. *Evaluation of NHS Direct first wave sites. Second interim report to the Department of Health.* Sheffield: Medical Care Research Unit, School of Health and Related Research, University of Sheffield, 2000.

[13] Pearce K, Rosen R. *NHS Direct. Learning from the London experience.* London: King's Fund, 2000.

[14] Airey C, Bruster S, Erens B, Lilley S-J, Pickering K, Pitson L. *The national surveys of NHS patients. General practice 1998: a survey carried out for the NHS Executive.* London: Department of Health, 1999.

[15] Carson D and Review Team. *Raising standards for patients. New partnerships in out-of-hours care. An independent review of GP out-of-hours services in England.* London: Department of Health, 2000.

[16] Milburn A. *NHS Direct set to be 'as well known as 999'.* Department of Health, Press Release 2000/0679.

[17] Hartley J. Can NHS Direct handle out-of-hours demand? *GP* 2000; 17 November.

[18] http://www.doh.gov.uk/nhswalkincentres/questions.htm

[19] http://www.doh.gov.uk/nhswalkincentres/info.htm

[20] Clews G. One step at a time. *BMJ* 2000; News review; 27 May: 18–20.

[21] Jones M. Lessons from Canada. *BMJ* 2000; 321: 928–31.

[22] Hutchison B. The place of walk-in clinics in healthcare systems. Uncertainty about impact demands careful evaluation and policy making. *BMJ* 2000; 321: 909–10.

[23] Salisbury C, Dale J, Hallam J, editors. *24-hour primary care.* Oxford: Radcliffe Medical Press, 1999.

[24] Iliffe S, Haig U. The future of general practice: out of hours work in general practice. *BMJ* 1991; 302: 1584–86.

[25] NPCRDC. *GP co-operatives and primary care emergency centres: organisation and impact.* Manchester: University of Manchester, National Primary Care Research and Development Centre, 1998.

[26] Salisbury C. Evaluation of a general practice out of hours co-operative. *BMJ* 1997; 314: 182–86 and 1598–99.

[27] Shipman C, Payne F, Hooper J, Dale J. Patient satisfaction with out-of-hours services: how do GP co-operatives compare

with deputizing and practice-based arrangements? *Journal of Public Health Medicine* 2000; 22 (2): 149–54.

[28] Bhanot S. Will we lose the valuable human touch? *Pulse* 2000; 15 December: 47.

[29] Drummond N, McConnachie A, O'Donnell C, Moffat K J, Wilson P, Ross S. Social variations in reasons for contacting general practice out-of-hours: implications for daytime service provision? *British Journal of General Practice* 2000; 50: 460–64.

[30] Salisbury C. Out-of-hours care: ensuring accessible high quality care for all groups of patients. *British Journal of General Practice* 2000; 50: 443–44.

[31] Shipman C, Addington-Hall J, Barclay S, Briggs J, Cox I, Daniels L, Millar D. Providing palliative care in primary care: how satisfied are GPs and district nurses with current out-of-hours arrangements. *British Journal of General Practice* 2000; 50: 477–78.

[32] Iliffe S. Nursing and the future of primary care. *BMJ* 2000; 320: 1020–21.

[33] Howie J G R, Heaney D J, Maxwell M. *Measuring quality in general practice.* RCGP Paper 75. London: Royal College of General Practitioners, 1997.

[34] Dixon J. *What is the hard evidence on the performance of 'mainstream' health services serving deprived and non-deprived areas in England?* London: The Stationery Office,

2000.

[35] De Maeseneer J, Hjordahl P, Starfield B. Fix what's wrong, not what's right with general practice in Britain. *BMJ* 2000; 320: 1616–67.

[36] Berliner H. US healthcare. America on the line. *Health Service Journal* 1998; 29 January: 28–29.

Chapter 3: Improving the quality of primary care services: will clinical governance meet expectations?

Rebecca Rosen

Introduction

This chapter examines the early impact of the introduction of clinical governance and considers its likely future effect on the quality of primary care services. After defining the meaning of clinical governance, Section 1 will outline a range of conceptual problems with assessing quality in primary care. It will also provide a brief overview of experience gained from work to improve primary care services prior to the 1997 NHS White Paper. Section 2 provides an overview of recent clinical governance activity in primary care, while Section 3 focuses on one specific aspect of clinical governance work – the management of poor performance. Section 4 explores how far clinical governance in primary care is likely to succeed in its aim of improving service quality.

What is clinical governance?

A first class service[1] defines clinical governance as 'a framework through which NHS organisations are accountable for continuously improving the quality of their services and safeguarding high standards of care by creating an environment in which excellence in clinical care will flourish'.

Various authors highlight different parts of the spectrum of activity necessary for effective clinical governance. These include quality improvement work aimed at individual clinicians, clinical teams and whole organisations;[2] explicit accountability mechanisms for quality improvement in primary care;[3] and the practical tasks required for clinical governance, such as audit, risk management, education and training, and implementation of national guidance (e.g. national service frameworks).[4]

In this chapter clinical governance will be considered as an umbrella term for the wide range of quality improvement activities noted above. It overlaps with (and may subsume) the implementation of other current policy initiatives and regulatory frameworks, such as NICE guidance, national service frameworks and health and safety legislation.

Crucially, it also requires less tangible developments, such as changes in the interrelationships between clinicians and in their values and attitudes – often referred to as 'cultural' changes. One of the main effects of such change is intended to be a more open and reflective approach to clinical practice. This would permit constructive, comparative review of clinical performance between clinicians, facilitating another key element of clinical governance – the early identification and management of poor clinical performance. This aspect of clinical governance will be discussed in some detail in Section 3 because of the level of political and media attention it has attracted.

Section 1. The context for clinical governance work in primary care

Any analysis of the impact of clinical governance must

recognise the difficulty of defining and assessing quality in primary care, and acknowledge that numerous quality improvement initiatives were already underway when the concept of clinical governance was launched in the 1997 NHS White Paper.

Conceptual difficulties in defining and measuring quality

The meaning of quality in primary care is hard to define because of the many roles that primary care aims to fulfil. In Toon's examination of 'good general practice'[5] he distinguishes three different approaches: a disease-focused biomedical model; a patient-focused humanist model; and a population-focused public health model. Toon's argument that the meaning of good general practice differs between models goes some way to explaining the variety of approaches to assessing and improving quality that have been put forward.

Working from a humanist perspective, Howie *et al.*[6] consider the nature of the doctor–patient interaction and its effect on a patient's ability to understand and cope with his/her condition as an essential determinant of quality. This highly intangible aspect of primary care is particularly difficult to quantify, though Howie *et al.* have tried to measure it through their 'patient enablement score'.

Their work draws attention to the difficulties of 'measuring' quality in primary care and the danger that by focusing on service developments with easily measurable outcomes, less tangible and harder-to-measure aspects of good general practice may be under-valued. This problem is particularly relevant to the use of NHS high-level performance indicators introduced in 1998. These indicators draw on routine data to allow rapid performance assessment at a population level in several important areas of primary care (e.g. cervical smear coverage). However, such measures pay no attention to the quality of the doctor–patient relationship, or to the psychosocial functions that, for some authors, lie at the heart of high quality British general practice.[7]

Taking a different approach, Greenhalgh and Eversley explore several different perspectives from which to consider quality in general practice.[8] They distinguish patient activity and performance, evidence-based, educational and managerial perspectives, each of which focuses on a different cluster of markers of quality. Importantly, Greenhalgh and Eversley argue that no single perspective can be used to describe the quality of care in practice. In a similar vein, Toon argues that it is impossible to define a single version of good quality general practice if there is no agreement as to what it is aiming to do and the values pursued through it.[5]

These points are of relevance to primary care groups and trusts (PCG/Ts), whose key tasks have been defined as developing primary care services, commissioning health care and improving the health of the local population. This combination of individual- and population-focused work needs to be reflected in the range of clinical governance activity undertaken. A balance will be needed between population goals such as improving access to services and work to improve the care of individual patients. The balance that is currently achieved will be explored in Section 2.

Prior work on quality improvement in primary care
The range of activity covered by the term 'clinical governance'

reflects multiple influences on our understanding of quality and the many quality improvement initiatives already underway when policy on clinical governance was developed. This work provides valuable lessons for those now implementing clinical governance, and has also raised important questions about how best to develop it.

Studies of variations in practice, and the limited research base for many interventions[9,10,11] stimulated the development of evidence-based medicine throughout the 1980s and 1990s. Effectiveness has become a defining characteristic of high quality care, and evidence-based guidelines and primary care audit programmes are central elements of clinical governance. Many motivated practices and primary care teams have already gained experience of audit and guideline implementation, but work to date has also highlighted problems with this work. Considerable support (both human and financial) is needed, particularly for smaller and non-computerised practices; confusion over aims, participants and audit topics has reduced the acceptance and impact of audit by clinicians,[12] and audit cycles have often remained un-completed. PCG/Ts will need to make difficult decisions about the extent to which they prioritise audit, the resources they allocate to it and how to ensure well-designed audits result in clinical change.

The contribution of organisational development to quality improvement has also been increasingly recognised since the mid-1980s. Improved access to primary care services, shorter waiting times, good communication and good practice organisation are increasingly seen as essential elements of high quality primary care.[4]

The need for on-going organisation-wide development to improve service quality is central to the work of authors such as Donald Berwick,[13] whose emphasis on continuous, reflective, organisational change is consistent with a total quality management approach to clinical governance. Here too, questions are raised for PCG/Ts. What balance should be obtained between this general and continuous approach to quality improvement and what is sometimes called the 'bad apple' approach of identifying and managing clinicians, teams and practices that perform particularly badly?

A range of government reports during the 1990s, and the 1996 White Paper *Delivering the future*,[14] identified other factors affecting the quality of primary care services, particularly in London. These include the poor quality of many practice premises,[15,16] weaknesses in current arrangements for education and training in primary care,[17] problems with recruiting and retaining general practitioners and community and practice nurses,[16] and the inflexibility of the contract of employment for general practitioners.[14]

These papers had already triggered much innovation prior to the introduction of clinical governance, although much still remains to be done. These include programmes of investment in practice premises, new approaches to education and training for primary care teams, and the introduction of a range of innovative services in the form of personal medical services (PMS) pilot projects.

Key proposals in *The NHS Plan*[18] relating to clinical governance include new systems for reporting and investigating adverse events and the new National Clinical

Assessment Authority, set up to investigate serious allegations of poor performance among individual clinicians. In addition, plans to fund improvements in over 3000 GP premises will complement the quality improvement plans of a cluster of London PCG/Ts for which poor premises are a particular local problem. The commitment to improve IT facilities in GP practices will also improve capacity for effective clinical governance. And proposals to employ more doctors and nurses on better pay scales could benefit services for which staff recruitment problems jeopardise quality.

In combination, these prior developments have created a strong foundation for clinical governance work. Much has already been learned about audit, changing clinical behaviour, organisational development and new models for providing primary care. But apart from the obligation to undertake audit – not always fulfilled by clinicians – other quality improvement initiatives have occurred piecemeal, resulting in patchy coverage and continued variations in the quality of primary care. Current policy on clinical governance requires a broad quality improvement agenda to be pursued on a universal basis.

Section 2. Current initiatives in implementing clinical governance

Early guidance on how to implement clinical governance came in the form of a health services circular outlining four key tasks for completion during 1999/2000.[19] Almost two years after its introduction, evidence about the implementation of clinical governance in primary care reveals variable resources available, many different approaches to its implementation and a wide range of priorities being pursued by PCG/Ts.

Resources

The National Tracker Survey of 72 PCGs and five first wave PCTs around the country[20] (see also footnote[1]) revealed that only 22 (44 per cent) out of 51 respondents had allocated budgets for clinical governance, ranging from £3000 to £150,000 (median £15,000). PCG leads feel they need more staff and IT resources, and noted limited time and money as key barriers to the development of clinical governance.

Monitoring progress

High quality data and good information systems and IT infrastructure will be essential for monitoring progress in clinical governance. In their exploration of evidence-based performance indicators for primary care, McColl *et al.* found that data on only eight out of 26 performance markers could be obtained in all of the GP practices in the study PCG, and only three practices could produce a complete data set.[21] Some PCG/Ts and practices are prioritising IT development,[22,23] but problems with incompatible computer systems and limited data entry skills are considerable,[24] and harmonised data collection systems may take years to develop.[22]

Proposed methods for monitoring progress in clinical governance include use of prescribing data, generic or composite quality indicators, referrals or admissions data, and measures of access to primary care.[20]

---

[1] *The National Tracker Survey of Primary Care Groups and Trusts* is being undertaken jointly by researchers from the National Primary Care Research and Development Centre and the King's Fund.

Early approaches to clinical governance work

A review of the baseline assessments from London PCG/Ts revealed diverse approaches to clinical governance, ranging from a PCG-wide focus on a single clinical topic through to a comprehensive range of clinical and organisational quality improvement activities.[25] Many PCGs have used their first year to develop the inter-professional relationships and trust required for effective clinical governance.[20]

Some PCG/Ts are providing a strong lead for clinical governance, identifying priorities at board level and assisting local practices to participate in the work. Others have used practice visits and consultative workshops to build consensus and identify priorities. A few are maintaining a light touch and encouraging practices to identify their own clinical governance priorities.

Despite clear guidance that clinical governance work should include a wide range of activities, many PCG/Ts have opted for simple first steps based around the often familiar territory of clinical audit. Seventy per cent of respondents to the Audit Commission survey of PCG development[26] said their first year's work involved an audit of treatment or referral for one or more HImP topics (coronary heart disease and diabetes most commonly). Only one-third of groups were planning to develop standard protocols across agencies and only one in eight were planning to focus on a specific care group (such as older people).

The National Tracker Survey also noted that much early clinical governance work has related to logistical and organisational development. In terms of specific priority topics, many of these had been identified by the PCG/T itself, with or without reference to the local HImP or local practices. Priority areas included prescribing, reducing hospital waiting lists and chronic disease management – where CHD was the most common disease identified. Only two reported their clinical governance priorities were linked to NICE guidance.

Accountability for clinical governance

Few details have yet emerged about the ways in which PCG/Ts will be accountable for their clinical governance work. In contrast to acute and community trusts, general practitioners are self-employed and employ many of their practice staff directly. There are thus no direct managerial lines of accountability between individual practices and the PCG board.

Allen distinguishes between vertical (upwards to the local health authority), horizontal (to other primary care group clinicians) and downwards accountability (to service users). She exemplifies upward accountability in the form of accountability agreements between a PCG and its local health authority. In some PCG/Ts, some of these agreements relate to clinical governance priorities such as diabetes and heart disease.[27] Initially, however, it is the horizontal accountability between peers – requiring a willingness to share information about one's own practice with colleagues – that is essential for establishing effective clinical governance work.

Allen also notes that, while some PCG/Ts have included their lay member on the clinical governance sub-committee, there is little evidence of involvement of the wider public in the development of downwards accountability for clinical governance. Most PCG/Ts are pursuing multiple aims for clinical governance work with very limited resources, and Allen argues that few are likely to prioritise the development of downwards accountability in the near future.

Clinical governance in non-medical professions

For nurses and the professions allied to medicine, the introduction of clinical governance also builds on many years of quality improvement work. The Royal College of Nursing has been leading quality improvement projects since the mid-1980s, through initiatives such as the dynamic standard setting system[28] and mechanisms for clinical supervision and reflective practice.[29] The College of Optometrists and the Royal Pharmaceutical Society have established programmes of continuing education and standards for professional practice for opticians and pharmacists respectively.

As intermediate care develops and more community-based multi-disciplinary teams are established, there will be a growing need for joint governance work.[30] The Royal Pharmaceutical Society has issued clear guidance on mechanisms for professional development and quality improvement. They also emphasise the need to develop clinical governance in close collaboration with other local health services through local links with pharmaceutical governance leads.[31]

Section 3. Managing poor performance in primary care

Regular media coverage concerning malpractice and professional misconduct has resulted in a policy focus on improving the identification and management of poor clinical performance. Although this is a core part of clinical governance work,[19] a number of conceptual problems have to be addressed if this work is to be developed effectively.

Conceptual problems with identifying poor performance

Foremost is the problem of defining poor performance. In their thorough review of poorly performing GPs, Rotherham et al.[32] considered under-performance with reference to practice development planning, health authority information sources, complaints, informal expressions of concern, patient views and self-identification. Each of these markers is argued to have strengths and weaknesses in terms of obtaining and interpreting information about performance. The consultation paper Supporting doctors, protecting patients[33] identified four categories of poor performance: serious clinical mistakes, failures in clinical performance, professional misconduct and failure to meet contractual commitments.

It remains unclear what constitutes a serious clinical mistake in primary care, where outcomes such as death and disability are relatively rare. In relation to 'failure of clinical performance', Rotherham et al. argue that repeated failures may be more telling than a single mistake.[32] There is also no clear standard against which 'failures' can be judged. Variations in referral and treatment rates are well recognised, but it is often hard to link observed rates to conclusions about good or bad practice.

Statements on good medical practice have been produced by the General Medical Council[34] and the Royal College of General Practitioners/General Practitioners Committee (RCGP/GPC),[35] but many grey areas remain. For example, as general practitioners are encouraged to take on more procedures (e.g. minor surgery), could complications associated with the learning curve[36] count as poor practice? What of situations where poor practice arises at least partly because of organisational failures (e.g. poor communication or inadequate resources to train team members for new roles)?

A further question relates to the role of complaints in identifying poor performance. RCGP/GPC guidance considers co-operating with the investigation of complaints as part of good practice, and unacceptable practice as hindering such investigation. Where explicit standards exist (e.g. for waiting times), complaints may be easily assessed, but softer issues such as 'open communication with patients' (one of the RCGP generic standards for good practice) are much harder to assess and may reflect legitimate differences in the personality and practice style of GPs. At what point might complaints about a surly but technically competent doctor be seen as poor performance? And what of a charming but technically weak GP who is popular with patients?

Given these many grey areas, it is difficult to define *precise* standards against which to identify poor performance in primary care. Furthermore, most GPs will continue, for the time being, to practice as independent contractors whose membership of the local PCG lacks formal management arrangements and direct lines of managerial accountability. This will make it harder for PCG/Ts to obtain information – beyond routine referral and prescribing data and local audit data – on GPs about whom concerns exist.

Having said this, several of the proposals in *Assuring the quality of medical practice*[37] may help to make problems more transparent to PCG/Ts. These include annual appraisals for all doctors, including locums, as a core requirement of clinical governance. Furthermore, the development of professional revalidation (see below) will also assist PCG/T efforts to identify and manage poor performance. Several authors have argued that mechanisms for revalidation will complement clinical governance work.[38,39] While it remains unclear exactly what revalidation will involve and if and how the findings could be made available to PCG/Ts, there is scope for both strands of work to identify failing doctors *before* serious problems occur and to use the local clinical governance system to offer early support.

Emerging mechanisms for identifying and managing poor performance

PCG/Ts are developing plans for dealing with poorly performing practices. Many are thinking about poorly performing teams as much as individual clinicians.[21] Indeed, Irvine notes that the need for collective responsibility for poor performance by all practice or clinical team members is increasingly acknowledged.[40] Most PCG/Ts are developing informal approaches to managing poor practices, such as informal discussion, audit and information dissemination, with a few considering more punitive measures, such as withdrawal of resources or disciplinary procedures.[20]

As independent practitioners, GPs have not had to undergo appraisal or peer review in the past. Complaints that cannot be handled within a practice are currently referred to the local health authority, where they are investigated and dealt with in conjunction with the local medical committee. Pilot schemes in the Trent Region have extended this performance review process to include a medical audit advisory group member and somebody involved in training and education.[41] The panel investigates complaints or concerns, conducts an assessment visit, and proposes local remedial action where possible. With few such pilot sites in existence, few GPs have experience of the constructive appraisal of under-performing colleagues and many express a reluctance to take on this role.

Although revalidation procedures are still under development in all specialities, their broad aim will be to assess clinicians' continued fitness to practice. They are likely to combine annual appraisal, based on participation in a cluster of activities (such as audit and continuing professional development) aimed at maintaining high standards of care, with periodic review by an external revalidation group.[42] It remains unclear who will conduct the annual appraisal of general practitioners and what their relationship with PCG clinical governance leads will be. Recognising the importance of preserving confidentiality in this delicate area, there may nevertheless be some potential to share information obtained through the two processes to facilitate early action if problems arise.

Given that involvement in audit and continuing professional development (CPD) are central to clinical governance and will be required for revalidation, these two developments should act synergistically to create a strong incentive for doctors to participate in such work. Ideally, this will facilitate the identification of poor performance at an early stage, before major clinical or behavioural problems have occurred. As PCG/Ts struggle to develop a role in relation to the identification and management of poor performance, a key challenge will be to develop links between clinical governance work and revalidation processes, and to take prompt and supportive action if such work reveals evidence of poor performance.

Complementary to the appraisal and revalidation systems through which poor performance may be identified at local level is the introduction of the new National Clinical Assessment Authority. Where serious problems are identified, the Authority will, 'provide a rapid and objective expert assessment of individual doctors' performance, recommending remedial action' to be co-ordinated locally.[37] At a local level, health authority powers will be strengthened through arrangements to screen professional staff qualifications and check for poor performance prior to appointment, and to strengthen their power to regulate, suspend and remove GPs, including locums, from their lists.[37]

In the document *The future of professionally led regulation*,[43] the RCGP/GPC propose a partnership model for the regulation of doctors, in which the medical profession plays a key role. The proposals emphasise the need for a clear 'diagnosis' of the problem under scrutiny, since under-performance may be due to poor individual practice or to local circumstances, such as deprivation or under-resourcing. Details of processes for remedial action and re-training remain sketchy but are to be professionally led. They are recognised to be resource intensive, given the need both to provide support for the doctor and continuing care for his or her patients. However, *The NHS Plan* offers a commitment to provide extra funding to fulfil the requirements of revalidation.

Section 4. Will clinical governance improve service quality in primary care?
This brief review of recent clinical governance work has highlighted the varied ways in which policy on quality improvement is being implemented in primary care. What conclusions can one draw about its early impact?

Confusing terminology?
The term 'clinical governance' has both helped and hindered quality improvement work in primary care. For many of those who are immersed in clinical governance work and leading its implementation, use of this umbrella term has improved understanding about the diverse factors that determine service quality and galvanised this thinking into a wide range of innovative action. However, members of some of the GP practices and primary care teams – whose participation is essential for effective clinical governance – still remain confused about the meaning of the term.

A bewildering array of policy initiatives overlap with and form part of clinical governance. The need to comply with national service frameworks and NICE guidance, PCG/T priorities and practice- or team-based quality improvement initiatives risks overloading and confusing practitioners. A key challenge for clinical governance leads is to 'interpret' clinical governance locally and motivate clinicians to participate in a manageable range of clinical governance work.

Limited resources
Resources remain a constraint on progress. The additional funding for professional development, practice premises and information technology pledged in *The NHS Plan* will help

with the development of clinical governance, but has not yet worked its way into the system. The National Tracker Survey and Audit Commission report describe ten-fold variations between the average and the highest budgets for clinical governance in PCG/Ts.[20,26] This must cover both the administrative costs of clinical governance (e.g. locum fees for lead clinicians) and quality improvement activities for local practitioners. These differences reflected the variability in overall management resources available to different PCG/Ts.[20]

Differences are also emerging in relation to funding for education and training, with some PCG/Ts pooling all resources to support a co-ordinated approach to training in clinical governance priority areas and others reliant upon multiple-fragmented funding sources.

The commitment in *The NHS Plan* to improve IT facilities in GP surgeries is also important for clinical governance, but must be matched by a commitment at local level to train and support clinicians in using such facilities. Few PCG/Ts have identified IT development as a clinical governance priority.[20,25]

Integrating clinical governance work

Research to date demonstrates variability in the extent to which clinical governance is integrated with the wider work of PCG/Ts (see Section 2). For some, clinical governance and health improvement priorities are one and the same, and underpinned by PCG/T investment priorities. Others have identified locally relevant priorities unrelated to NSFs or the HImPs through which to develop interest and participation in clinical governance.

If clinical governance is to work as a framework for the continuous improvement of local services, priorities will need to be integrated with wider PCG/T policies – particularly HImPs and investment plans. Within teams and practices, clinical governance will need to underpin development plans and function across multi-disciplinary teams. This will become increasingly important as more intermediate care projects are established involving primary and secondary health and social care agencies.

Multi-professional collaboration is now common in terms of guideline development and implementation. However, experience of wider inter-professional quality assurance is limited and will require innovative approaches to data collection, peer review, and joint education and training. Gillam *et al.* note that hierarchy, gender and varied educational achievements among team members can all act as barriers to effective multi-disciplinary learning.[44]

Cultural change and the early identification of poor performance

Considerable efforts are being made to involve local practitioners and develop the open culture and trusting relationships between practitioners and PCG/Ts required for effective clinical governance. These changes are essential to achieve some of its key aims: accountability between primary care practitioners and their PCG board; learning through open discussion of clinical problems; and the early identification and management of poor performance.

Intensive contact with practices and clinicians and on-going support from clinical governance leads are encouraging participation in clinical governance. Some PCG/Ts report that *all* local doctors are participating in audits and see this as a first step to developing a wider clinical governance agenda. Moreover, non-participation in clinical governance work may act as a first warning sign of problem practices requiring further investigation by the clinical governance team.

The overlap between clinical governance and revalidation requirements will lead most clinicians to have at least limited involvement in clinical governance work. It remains unclear, though, how PCG/Ts will encourage reluctant clinicians and practices to engage in wider activities, nor how they will deal with them if they refuse.

The emerging relationship between revalidation teams, clinician appraisers and clinical governance leads will be essential to avoid duplication and ensure early detection of problems. Although *Assuring the quality of medical practice* goes some way to clarifying the roles of different organisations in respect of poor performance, it offers little guidance on how to integrate these different strands of quality improvement activity, and the detail still needs to be worked out at a local level.[37]

Moreover, such links may well generate potential problems. Rotherham *et al.* stress that effective systems for managing poor performance need confidentiality, partnership with the profession, leadership by a senior person and fair transparent processes. How will confidentiality be maintained if information is transferred between these teams? Where a PCG/T clinical governance lead is young and inexperienced, will he or she command the respect required for such work?

What should be the role of lay people on clinical governance committees in this sensitive area of work?

Resources will also be a potential stumbling block for the effective management of poor performance. If this work is to succeed in its preventive aim of detecting problems early, it will be essential to offer certain clinicians support and re-training before they require referral to higher authorities. With the limited clinical governance funds available to most PCG/Ts (see Section 2), how will they prioritise such work compared to their main clinical governance priorities? What would be the effect on the wider professional community of identifying problem doctors (clinicians) without being able to fund the help they need?

What to do and how to measure progress?

It remains too early to judge which clinical governance priorities and which methods will result in the greatest improvements in service quality. Leadership skills and resources will be two key determinants of success, although evidence is lacking on whether PCG or practice level leadership are more important for enrolling local practitioners in clinical governance work.

Advances in methods for multi-disciplinary training are also needed if clinical governance is to succeed, but little is known about how best to promote learning in such situations. Equally, it remains unclear whether pooling money from several sources (education and training, IT, modernisation and general management funds) into a central clinical governance budget will be the most effective way to fund quality improvement work. A key challenge will be to learn quickly from PCG/Ts that seem to be succeeding. The emerging system of beacon practices,[45] access to the National Electronic Library for Health, and opportunities for peer learning such as the primary care collaborative and clinical governance networks, will aid dissemination.

There are no simple measures of progress in clinical governance by which to monitor its overall impact. Many PCG/Ts deliberately spent the first year developing an organisational infrastructure for clinical governance, so it may be only those which prioritised audits or disease registers that will be in a position to measure changes in clinical outcomes arising from their clinical governance work.

Will the pace of change be sufficient to meet public expectation?

The changes required for effective clinical governance will take many years to achieve. Many PCG/Ts are arranging practice visits, clinical governance conferences and workshops to build involvement and learning, but progress is generally slow.

Few PCG/Ts report having strategies on how to manage clinicians who do not participate in clinical governance work. Evidence from national comparative audits in the acute sector suggests that this 'softly, softly' approach does win support and participation from sceptical clinicians over time.[46]

However, against a backdrop of growing public scepticism about professional self-regulation, the rate of development of effective clinical governance in primary care and associated mechanisms for accountability are unlikely to allay the concerns of politicians, the public and the media. The pressures on primary care professionals in this regard are likely to intensify.

References

[1] Department of Health. *A first class service.* London: Department of Health, 1998.

[2] Royal College of General Practitioners. *Clinical governance: practical advice for primary care in England and Wales.* London: RCGP, 1999.

[3] Baker R, Likhani M, Fraser R, Cheater F. A model for clinical governance in primary care groups. *BMJ* 1999; 318: 779–83.

[4] Roland M, Holden J, Campbell S. *Quality assessment for general practice: supporting clinical governance in PCGs.* Manchester: National Primary Care Research and Development Centre, University of Manchester, 1998. www.npcrdc.man.ac.uk/

[5] Toon P. *What is good general practice?* London: Royal College of General Practitioners, Occasional paper, 1994.

[6] Howie J G, Heaney D J, Maxwell M. *Measuring quality in general practice. Pilot study of needs, process and outcome measure.* London: Royal College of General Practitioners, Occasional paper, 1997.

[7] Fugelli P, Heath I. The nature of general practice. *BMJ* 1996; 312: 456–57.

[8] Greenhalgh T, Eversley J. *Quality in general practice.* London: King's Fund, 1999.

[9] Wennberg J. On the need for outcomes research and the prospects for evaluative clinical sciences. In: Andersen T and Mooney G, editors. *The challenges of medical practice variations.* Economic Issues in Health Care Series. London: Macmillan Press, 1990.

[10] Eddy D. Variations in physician practice: the role of uncertainty. *Health Affairs* 1984; 3: 74–89.

[11] Cochrane A L. *Effectiveness and efficiency: random reflections on health services.* London: Royal Society of Medicine Press, 1964.

[12] Hopkins A. Clinical audit: time for reappraisal? *J. Roy. Coll. Phys.* 1996; 30 (5): 415–24.

[13] Berwick D. A primer on the improvement of health services. *BMJ* 1996 312: 619–22.

[14] Department of Health. *Primary care: delivering the future.* London: HMSO, 1996.

[15] Tomlinson B (chairman). *Report of the inquiry into London's health service, medical education and research.* London: HMSO, 1992.

[16] Turnberg L. *Health service in London: a strategic review.* London: Department of Health, 1998.

[17] Chief Medical Officer. *A review of continuing professional development in primary care.* London: Department of Health, 1998.

[18] Department of Health. *The NHS Plan. A plan for investment. A plan for reform.* Cm No. 4818-I. London: HMSO, 2000.

[19] NHS Executive. *Clinical governance: quality in the new NHS.* HSC1999/065. Leeds: NHS Executive, 1999.

[20] Wilkin D, Gillam S, Leese B. *The national tracker survey of primary care groups and trusts: progress and challenges 1999–2000.* Manchester: NPCRDC/King's Fund, 2000.

[21] McColl A, Roderick P, Smith H, Wilkinson E, Moore M, Exworthy M, Gabbay J. Clinical governance in primary care groups: the feasibility of deriving evidence-based performance indicators. *Qual. Health Care* 2000; 9 (2): 90–97.

[22] Lamont P, Murphy P, Singleton S. A response from Northumberland MEDICS. *BMJ* 2000; e-letter, 20 Oct. www.bmj.com/cgi/content/full/321/7265/871#responses.

[23] Ayres I *et al.* Clinical governance in primary care groups. *Public Health Medicine* 1999; 2: 47–52.

[24] McColl A, Roland M. Knowledge and information for clinical governance. *BMJ* 2000; 321 (7265): 871–74.

[25] Wye L, Rosen R, Dewar S. *Clinical governance in primary care: a review of baseline assessments*. London: King's Fund, 2000.

[26] Audit Commission. *The PCG agenda: early progress of PCGs in 'The new NHS'*. London: Audit Commission, 2000.

[27] Allen P. Accountability for clinical governance: developing collective responsibility for quality in primary care. *BMJ* 2000; 321: 608–11

[28] Morrell C, Harvey G, Kitson A. Practitioner based quality improvement: a review of the RCN's dynamic standard setting system. *Quality in Health Care* 1997; 6: 29–34.

[29] Royal College of Nursing. *Guidance for nurses on clinical governance*. London: RCN, 1998.

[30] College of Optometrists. *Professional guidance on clinical governance*. London: College of Optometrists, 2001. www/college-optometrists.org/professional/clingov.htm

[31] Royal Pharmaceutical Society. *Achieving excellence in pharmacy through clinical governance*. London: RPS, 2000.

[32] Rotherham, G, Martin D, Joesbury H, Mathers N. *Measures to assist GPs whose performance gives cause for concern*. Sheffield: ScHARR, 1997.

[33] Chief Medical Officer for England. *Supporting doctors, protecting patients*. London: HMSO, 1999.

[34] The General Medical Council. *Good medical practice.* London: GMC, 1998.

[35] Royal College of General Practitioners and General Practitioners Committee. *Good medical practice for general practitioners.* London: October 1999.

[36] Smith R. All changed, changed utterly. *BMJ* 1998; 316: 1917–18.

[37] NHS Executive. *Assuring the quality of medical practice.* Leeds: NHS Executive, 2000.

[38] Pringle M. Clinical governance in primary care: participating in clinical governance. *BMJ* 2000; 321: 737–40.

[39] McColl A, Roland M. Clinical governance in primary care: knowledge and information for clinical governance. *BMJ* 2000; 321: 871–74.

[40] Irvine, D. The performance of doctors II: maintaining good practice, protecting patients from poor performance. *BMJ* 1997; 314: 1613–19.

[41] Moore W. Back from the brink. *Health Services Journal* 1999; 22 April: 24–27.

[42] General Medical Council. *Ensuring standards, securing the future.* London: GMC, 2000.

[43] Royal College of General Practitioners. *The future of professionally led regulation.* London: RCGP, 2000.

[44] Gillam S, Eversley J, Snell J, Wallace P. *Building bridges. The future of GP education – developing partnerships with the service.* London: King's Fund, 1999.

[45] NHS beacons web site: www.doh.gov.uk/nhsexec/beacons.htm

[46] Rosen, R. *The role of intervention registries and other clinical data sets in health care quality monitoring, research and technology assessment.* Report for the Department of Health Research and Development Directorate. London: London School of Hygiene and Tropical Medicine, 1998.

Chapter 4: The challenge of public involvement

Will Anderson

Why involve the public?

The involvement of patients, carers and the public in health and health care has never been a single coherent policy stream within the NHS. Politically, it is informed by diverse ideologies: consumerism, liberalism, radical democratic traditions. It embraces beliefs about civil society, State responsibilities, individual rights and autonomy. Consequently, the question *Why involve the public?* has many different answers, depending on individual values and interests.

The democratic case makes the strongest appeal to values rather than instrumental arguments. Public institutions ought to seek the involvement of both citizens and users in their decision-making because their legitimacy rests on the support of the public they serve. This is not simply a matter of political accountability. The sustenance of democracy requires that the relationships between a society's constituent parts are open and healthy. Thus, health service organisations that nurture fruitful relationships with their users and their local communities will prosper as part of those local communities, rather than remaining isolated professional providers.

This links to a more pragmatic case, which sees the improvement of the health of a population as necessarily requiring the participation of everyone concerned. Whether this is articulated as professional partnership with community stakeholders or as the community defining the agenda for professional action, there is a broad consensus that health services can no longer go it alone: that to achieve sustainable improvements in health, both for individuals and for communities, everyone's interests and contribution should be valued.[1]

This in turn leads to a straightforward argument for efficient use of resources: that only through a critical understanding of the health needs of communities will resources be best used to meet those needs. Although the identification of need has long been at the centre of the professional role, user and public involvement ensures that professional decision-making does not develop a momentum solely of its own but is constantly challenged by alternative perspectives on need. Re-framing the user–health professional relationship also has the potential to change patterns of dependency. Traditional approaches to meeting ever rising demand for care by increasing activity appear unsustainable.[2]

Finally, there is a strong consumerist argument, which sees public involvement as a way of ensuring not only that needs are met, but that needs are met in ways that are appropriate and sensitive to users and communities.

Overall, public involvement is about recognising and valuing the interests of one set of stakeholders in the NHS – its users and citizens. This does not mean that their interests should always hold sway. Like any organisation, the NHS is a political process in which all players negotiate their different claims to current and future practice and policy. Patients and local people have never had as strong a voice as other players, doctors in particular, in this process.[3] Broadly speaking, patient and public involvement initiatives are an attempt to redress the balance.

New Labour's political and social inheritance

In 1997, the replacement of a right-wing government by a more centrist administration may have raised hopes for new investment in public involvement activity in the NHS. In practice, much of what has happened in the last four years reflects the somewhat opportunistic flowering of the Conservative inheritance.

The Conservatives may have had little concern to address the 'democratic deficit' in the health service, but they were interested in re-thinking how the institutions and professions that make up the service worked, and consequently in how the role of the users of the service was defined. Two key changes were the introduction of the internal market and the shift to 'needs-led' commissioning of community care and, less directly, health services. Both of these changes challenged the traditional role of health and social care professionals in deciding who should get what. The institutional assumption of the post-war consensus – that the State should and could deliver welfare on the basis of professional expertise – was diminished.[4] At the front end, the difference made to patient experience may not have been great, but a process had begun of thinking more critically about how user interests are valued in the design and delivery of health and social care.

There were many specific initiatives in the first half of the 1990s that contributed to New Labour's inheritance. *The Patient's Charter* defined a set of consumer rights for health services users.

Local voices exploited the purchaser–provider split as an opportunity for health authorities to be champions of the people. The National NHS Patient Partnership strategy made the case for user and public involvement at both individual and corporate level. In different ways, these initiatives strengthened the hand of those at local level who wanted to change the ways in which health services related to their users and communities.

Wider social change has also left its mark on professional–lay relationships. The fragmentation of social institutions – marriage, the family, careers, professions, unions, churches, neighbourhoods, indeed all the elements of civil society – has broken many of the traditional bounds of individual identity. When professions and institutions of any kind no longer command automatic respect, the State needs to take greater care in weaving a social fabric that values the interests of all its constituent members. The Conservatives may have promoted this state of affairs through the determined individualism of their market ideology, but it was left to New Labour to begin the process of addressing it.

The priorities of New Labour

New Labour is undoubtedly committed to social inclusion, opportunities for all and the elimination of inequities in health and welfare, but its peculiar combination of populism and central control is not the ideal starting point for fostering greater user and public involvement in the process of change. Like its predecessor administration, New Labour is glad of its power and eager to hold on to it. Alan Milburn insists that 'the consumer is king' in the NHS, but consumer choices remain – as in a real market – constrained by the power and decision-making of the providers.

New Labour has not, however, completely lost its interest in democracy. Although the renewal of local government is controversial, there is a clear policy emphasis on increasing local accountability and involving local communities in council decision-making. This enthusiasm has spilled over into the NHS reforms, but does not quite know where to take hold. The NHS remains a vast professionally-dominated institution with a fragmented and idiosyncratic interface with local communities. It is still a hostile environment in which to nurture meaningful public involvement work. In this environment, it is much easier for the Government to focus on the patient as consumer rather than the patient as citizen. The former presents no radical challenges to the status quo, whereas the latter is altogether more risky. The Government may be happy for local government officials to listen harder to the people they serve, but the Department of Health is much more wary of upsetting the mass of health service professionals whose good humour it necessarily relies upon. Democratic renewal in the NHS is always going to be a struggle.

Policy initiatives

The new NHS: modern, dependable[5] defined a considerable agenda for change for primary care. The inclusion of the lay member on the new primary care groups (PCGs) was a marker of the direction in which policy was travelling. PCGs had to be more than the sum of their parts, i.e. of their GP practices and practice lists. They had to focus on the health of the whole of their local population and think about how improvements in health could be made in ways that went beyond the individual client relationships of each primary care professional. The inclusion of the lay member signalled, albeit in a rather simplistic way, the importance of PCG accountability to local communities.

Many lay members have struggled to shape meaningful and effective roles in PCGs. These difficulties have been unsurprising; as a symbolic focus of the policy shift planned for primary care, it is no wonder that many have found the tension between long-standing professional culture and broader community interests hard to live with.

The most comprehensive statement of the Government's commitment to public involvement in health care, *Patient and public involvement in the new NHS*[6] effectively drew together the various strands of NHS policy that addressed public involvement, including clinical governance, health improvement programmes, health action zones, user involvement in research, and patient and public information. Although this document was valuable as an explicit statement of government commitment to public involvement being 'strategically and systematically' built into the way NHS organisations operate, the lack of any detailed framework to achieve this aim gave the document an inescapably rhetorical feel. Nonetheless, the broader sweep of policy change in primary care was cited as the context for greater public involvement activity within PCGs:

Primary Care Groups (PCGs) are an essential part of the Government's programme of NHS reforms, working at local level to improve health, develop primary care and community services and advise on or commission a range of hospital services. It will be important that PCGs work with their local communities to develop shared goals and aims for improving local health and well being. This will help to promote openness, accountability and public confidence in the NHS.

Although this document had very little impact on PCGs – their priorities lay elsewhere – it was valuable as an explicit statement of the necessity of public involvement in a population and community-focused NHS. This is likely to be the basis of any real long-term commitment to public involvement by PCGs and other NHS organisations.

The NHS Plan,[7] rushed out in the Summer of 2000, appeared to go much further in defining mechanisms for involvement, but these mechanisms were poorly thought through and only very tenuously linked to the overall vision of the Plan. The Plan claimed a simple vision: 'a health service designed around the patient' in which 'services will be available when people require them, tailored to their individual needs'. Unfortunately, this vision is full of contradictions.

The service will be designed 'around' the patient, not by patients or with patients. Patient needs are assumed to be transparent, when in reality they are defined in the interaction of individuals with the service – and it is still predominantly professionals who decide what does and does not 'count' as a need worthy of intervention.

As before, the Plan's consumerist rhetoric manages to promote a patient-focused vision without significantly challenging the powers that control and deliver the service. The professionals remain in control, albeit with a brief to provide their product in ways that are more tuned to patient demand. The slow shift in the commercial world from providing product-led services to providing consumer-led services has found its way to the heart of the Government's thinking about the health service. But this does not mean that consumers actually *lead* services, only that services are designed with greater knowledge of consumer interests.

This consumerist vision sits uneasily with the new mechanisms of public involvement specified in the Plan. This has been particularly evident in discussions about the new Patient Advocacy and Liaison Service, which was conceived as a trust-run greeting and problem-solving service that also had to encompass an advocacy role (following the abolition of community health councils). This elision of consumer needs and citizen rights has been widely criticised by patient organisations.

Following the publication of the Plan, it rapidly became clear that none of the new mechanisms had been thought through in detail. If they are to succeed, their functions and powers will have to be made much clearer. There is a real risk that they will become high cost mechanisms of legitimation rather than real forces for change within the NHS.[8]

Progress in practice

There are many more drivers for change beyond the pronouncements of ministers and civil servants. Out in the broad field of primary care, opportunities are being taken. Prime among these has been the corporate opportunities of PCGs themselves. These half-way-house organisations – a point of transition between the eclectic leftovers of the last administration and the harsh realities of trust status – have provided primary care professionals with a clear corporate developmental agenda. No doubt many PCGs have felt their reality to be as harsh as anyone's in the NHS, but they have been free to pursue their responsibilities for health improvement, commissioning and primary care development without the full weight of governance responsibilities that autonomy demands (the PCT governance guidance runs to 170 pages).

The exercise of this freedom has been evident in PCGs' approaches to public involvement. Distanced from the daily grind of primary health care teams, PCGs have had a chance to explore the possibilities of public involvement, albeit constrained by the enormous demands on their time and resources of the organisational development agenda as a whole. In a recent study, three-quarters of PCG chief executives in London felt that public involvement was a high priority, although only 16 per cent identified public involvement as a higher-than-average priority relative to all their 'high priorities'.[9]

Above all, because PCGs are corporate bodies, there has been opportunity for the development, for the first time, of corporate commitment to public involvement in primary care. It has often been the lay member who has advocated for and led on public involvement, but recognition of the impossibility of one person fulfilling a representative community role has forced PCG boards to consider their corporate responsibilities in dealing with this issue. Thus, the weakness of a potentially marginalising mechanism instituted by the centre – the lay representative – has encouraged widespread debate about what a fuller corporate response might look like.

Without a clear framework with which to build a corporate strategy for public involvement, PCGs have been forced to draw on whatever local expertise and skills are available and do the best they can. The results have inevitably been very diverse, characterised by differences in aims, methods, audiences, settings, outputs and, inasmuch as these can be identified, outcomes. Much of this activity is still tentative and is unlikely to be challenging to the PCGs concerned. In particular, although there is considerable literature available about approaches and methods of public involvement, the mechanism of impact within and beyond the organisation remains poorly theorised and rarely thought through in practice. It is here that guidance is most needed, as it is this process that is easily neglected in favour of the front-end processes of engagement.

The adoption of corporate approaches to public involvement by PCGs may, in the best case scenario, herald a new era of 'community-oriented primary care'.[10] This is not a new idea, but one that may benefit from the new level of organisational support – although the challenges of community development are considerable and unfamiliar to most primary care professionals.[11]

There is, however, a contrary danger: that PCG corporacy distracts from the need to develop appropriate professional–lay relationships at practice level. In setting out to develop public involvement strategies, most PCGs have focused principally on establishing PCG-based initiatives or partnerships. Only a minority has been concerned with the development of practice-level initiatives. This illuminates a central problem for all PCGs: signing up the professionals in their constituent practices to the PCG organisational development agenda.

Education and training
The biggest challenge at practice level is not the development of

patient-participation groups (or other specific models), but getting the professionals and staff, particularly the GPs, to rethink the nature of their relationships with their patients. The enormous amount of work examining doctor–patient partnerships and shared decision-making has yet to filter through to many local primary health care teams. This may require a 'culture change', but acknowledging as much should not mean that the task is filed away with other interminably long-term organisational development objectives. Clinical governance provides PCGs with an obvious route into addressing this issue, although the size of this developmental agenda in itself means that medical priorities inevitably dominate.

Training programmes that specifically address the quality of clinician–patient relationships (such as the NHSE London Region's 'Preparing Professionals for Partnership with the Public' and the national 'Expert Patients Programme') should help bring about real change. Courses are appearing that aim to provide both health professionals and patients with skills in decision support. There is increasing international exchange of practical experience and resources in this area.[12]

The future for primary care
In the immediate future, the transformations needed at the sharp end of health care delivery are likely to be seriously overshadowed, as usual, by the demands of organisational change – above all by the inexorable metamorphosis of PCGs into PCTs. This change has considerable implications for public involvement activity. In particular, community-oriented lay members will soon be a thing of the past, replaced by non-executive directors with, as the PCT governance makes clear, 'critical detachment' from

the hurly-burly of delivery. This will be felt as a considerable loss by those PCGs that have benefited from hands-on lay members. PCG lay members may have been an ill-conceived way of seeking community accountability, but many have made the job into something creative and challenging for their PCGs. It will be interesting to see if PCTs are able to find new ways of tapping that creativity.

Yet, arguably, PCTs are the synthesis of the lay member–corporate dialectic that has bedevilled PCG approaches to public involvement. For one of the six key functions for which the PCT board is held accountable by the NHS Executive on behalf of the Secretary of State is:

> *to ensure that the Executive Committee leads an effective dialogue between the organisation and the local community on its plans and performance and that these are responsive to the community's needs.*[13]

Never has public involvement been so clearly written into the terms of governance of a NHS body. If the new non-executive directors want to ensure public involvement is taken seriously within PCTs, they have the clearest possible corporate terms on which to do this.

Conclusion

How are we to judge the progress made under the New Labour administration? Here are two possible perspectives.

First, from the perspective of history, New Labour has exploited effectively the consumerist Conservative legacy. The value of user and public views in shaping and improving services is widely accepted, at least at corporate PCG level. Public involvement is now a recognised component of the drive for efficiency and quality. There is no turning back: users and the public must be treated as real stakeholders in the modernisation of the health service.

Second, from the perspective of the typical patient and citizen, little has changed. Doctors still call the shots; opportunities for involvement in any significant decision-making are scarce; public board meetings are little more than *faits accomplis*; accountability to local people is negligible; and poor service remains extraordinarily difficult to challenge, let alone change. Genuine partnership remains a distant goal. There may be much afoot to tackle some of these problems, but the direction continues to come from above, not from below.

New Labour has not broken much new ground in public involvement. A more radical vision, with the resources to match, is unlikely to unfold in the business-like world of contemporary health care delivery. Nonetheless, New Labour remains a party of liberal democracy; consequently, there is space and opportunity for the diverse flowering of public involvement in primary care at local level – supporting slow but crucial changes in professional culture throughout the health service.

References

[1] Buggins E. People as partners: adopting the 'crabmatic vision' approach. *Community Practitioner* 2000; 73 (3): 525–26.

[2] Morrison I, Smith R. Hamster health care. *BMJ* 2000; 321: 1541–42.

[3] Brownlea A. Participation: myths, realities and prognosis. *Social Science and Medicine* 1987; 25 (6): 605–14.

[4] Langan M. The contested concept of need. In: Langan M, editor. *Welfare: needs, rights and risks*. London: Routledge, 1998.

[5] Secretary of State for Health: *The new NHS: modern, dependable*. London: Department of Health, 1997.

[6] Department of Health. *Patient and public involvement in the new NHS*. London: Department of Health, 1999.

[7] Secretary of State for Health: *The NHS Plan*. London: Department of Health, 2000.

[8] Harrison S, Mort M: Which champions, which people? Public and user involvement in health care as a technology of legitimation. *Social Policy and Administration* 1998; 32 (1): 60–70.

[9] Anderson W, Florin D. *Involving the public – one of many priorities*. London: King's Fund, 2000.

[10] Gillam S, Miller R. *A public health experiment in primary care – community oriented in primary care.* London: King's Fund, 1996.

[11] O'Keefe E, Hogg C. Public participation and marginalized groups: the community development model. *Health Expectations* 1999; 2: 245–54.

[12] Coulter A *et al. The Oxford forum on shared decision-making: advancing the theory and practice of shared decision-making.* London: Nuffield Trust, Final Report, July 2000.

[13] NHS Executive. *PCT corporate governance framework.* Leeds: NHS Executive, 2000.

Chapter 5: A new accountability for primary care?

Richard Lewis

The NHS is often described as 'publicly accountable'. At its highest level this means that the Secretary of State for Health is answerable to Parliament for the actions of every NHS agency (and by extension, every NHS worker). Of course, the operational mechanisms for holding the NHS to account are far more complex than this. This is particularly true of primary care, where one key group of professionals, GPs, are largely independent contractors (i.e. self-employed, with most holding an individual contract with the Secretary of State for Health), but who maintain a wide range of other relationships with other health agencies.

So what do we mean when we refer to 'accountability'? Accountability is a notoriously elusive term. Day and Klein (1987) identify a number of different types of accountability: 'political accountability', where those enjoying delegated authority are answerable for their actions to the people; 'managerial accountability', where those enjoying delegated authority are answerable for carrying out agreed tasks according to agreed criteria of performance; and 'professional accountability', where those with specialist skills account for their actions only to their peers (through a process of self-regulation).

Accountability is founded on a relationship that has, at its heart, a 'right of authority'. Those holding others to account have superior authority over those who are accountable.[1] At its simplest level, ministers are subordinate to the will of the people (represented by Parliament), and NHS agencies are subordinate to ministers. But, as Day and Klein point out, legitimate authority does not always convert into effective power; for accountability to go beyond the theoretical, *effective control* is a prerequisite. Accountability, therefore, places limits on autonomy (the ability of an individual or organisation to act without reference to a third party).

Predictably, in the 'real world' accountability is less clearly observed than the theory might suggest. Does a senior consultant consider her manager to enjoy superior authority within the hospital? How might a Secretary of State for Health hold to account more than 30,000 independently contracted GPs? And what informal lines of accountability (i.e. not enforceable through contractual or other systematic means) might exist between health workers? Importantly, accountabilities may conflict. For example, NHS bodies are accountable 'upwards' to ministers but are also accountable 'downwards' to the public that they directly serve.

The three types of accountability identified above do not all integrate into a seamless model, nor, in practice, are they easily separated. Managerial roles, far from simply the 'technical' execution of the will of political masters, often (if not always) involve a re-interpretation of policy ends as well as policy means. 'Bottom-up' theories of the policy process suggest that theoretical divisions between policy 'making' and its implementation are false (see for example De Roo and Maarse (1990) for a discussion of the role of implementers in the development of health policy[2]).

This chapter considers the accountability relationships of primary care professionals (mainly focusing on GPs). A question is posed – have the Labour government's health policies changed the way in which primary care is held to account? The focus of this chapter is on structures and processes that underpin the relationship between primary care and the wider NHS (for example, with health authorities and the NHS Executive). Other dimensions of accountability are clearly also important and are addressed in other chapters. Will Anderson considers the 'public involvement' agenda in relation to primary care and Rebecca Rosen addresses issues of 'personal' and 'professional' accountability within the context of clinical governance and professional self-regulation.

Background

Since the 1970s, governments have become increasingly interested in the public accountability of the NHS and, more particularly, in their ability to control its actions. This new focus emerged in response to economic retrenchment, leading to pressure on public finances, together with a growing instability in the post-war consensus over the role and scope of publicly-funded health services

Governments have experimented with the 'right' kind of accountability and performance management mechanisms. In particular, the power relationship between the 'centre' (government and NHS headquarters) and the 'periphery' (local health planners and service providers) has shifted to and fro, although the underlying tendency has been towards greater centralisation.[3] During the 1980s, the centre sought to exert its control through the introduction of hierarchical general management, tighter control of national and local cash-limited budgets, and the development and use of performance indicators. However, by and large this was limited to the hospital sector as the key component of NHS costs.

And yet, despite the growth in overt 'top-downism', the NHS of the 1980s was characterised by a failure to meet public expectations. The Thatcher government, dissatisfied with the apparent impotence of government to impose its will through managerial means, sought to introduce a new approach to cost containment and accountability. The 'internal market' that was introduced in 1990 superficially decentralised planning and decision-making, making them, in theory at least, subject to local factors of demand and supply (although it has been argued convincingly that central control remained undiminished[4]). While, to many, the internal market appeared a managerial revolution, the introduction and subsequent growth of GP fundholding involved front-line clinical staff in the planning and commissioning of services. This proved highly significant for primary care, challenging the historic general practice culture of autonomy and its virtual disengagement from wider health management.

Previous attempts to involve clinicians in health management had been limited to the operational management of hospital activity through the resource management initiative in hospital services.[5] GP fundholding sought to harness the gate-keeping role of GPs as a key part of its strategy for controlling costs and driving up service quality. GP fundholding spawned new variants such as total purchasing, introducing a greater emphasis on collective accountability that crossed the hitherto impervious boundary of the single general practice partnership.

New Labour, old policy

The in-coming Labour government, while proclaiming a 'new' NHS actually kept, and built on, many of the central tenets and characteristics of the previous regime.[6,7] This should not be wholly surprising. After all, Labour supported the 1997 *NHS (Primary Care) Act*, the final piece of legislation by the Major government. The role of primary care as prime agents of service planning and monitoring, already evolving under the Conservatives, was strengthened by Labour.

Clues to Labour's approach to the accountability of primary care can be found in their preoccupations while in opposition. For the Labour opposition, GP fundholding typified much of what was bad about Conservative health policy. In particular, they railed against the individualism that was peculiar to fundholding (with its subsequent 'two-tierism' and perceived fragmentation of service delivery) and considered it essentially 'unaccountable' to the public. These concerns were to be addressed through the introduction of a new type of primary care organisation, the primary care group (a chrysalis that would metamorphose into a primary care trust). These organisations were not wholly unfamiliar, and built on the structures that went before (see Chapter 1). However, *The NHS Plan* has signalled that the evolution of primary care organisations is not complete with its announcement that 'Care Trusts' are soon to be established. These trusts will integrate health and social care service provision, overcoming a structural division that has long impeded care planning for particular client groups, such as the elderly and children.

PCG/Ts are designed to incorporate primary care clinicians into the heart of the NHS decision-making process. Detailed guidelines for membership of PCG boards and PCT executive committees (the key decision-making bodies) have been laid down, ensuring a built-in majority for clinicians (and specifically for GPs if they so choose). In the case of free-standing PCTs, their ultimate governance lies with their boards (PCGs remain a semi-autonomous component of a health authority). These boards are led by a non-executive, lay chair appointed by the Secretary of State (although in future appointments they will be made by a new and independent NHS appointments commission) and must have a majority of lay, non-executive members. However, it has also been made clear that the clinically-dominated executive committee of the board is the 'engine room' of the PCT and is expected to lead on operational and strategic policy.[8]

PCG/Ts are subject to a range of new formal accountability structures. Both must produce annual accountability agreements setting out how they propose to fulfil their functions. In addition, they must produce primary care investment plans, clinical governance and annual reports. PCTs must also produce formal annual accounts and the chief executive is the accountable officer, ultimately accountable to Parliament. Both PCGs and PCTs are expected to contribute to, and be bound by, the local health improvement programmes (HImPs) that are drawn up by their local health authority.

What does the introduction of PCG/Ts tell us about the changing nature of the accountability of primary care? Three important themes emerge:

The collectivisation of primary care

Unlike the voluntary GP fundholding and total purchasing schemes, membership of PCG/Ts is automatic for all GPs and community nurses. This element of compulsion in the regulation of NHS–professional relations marks a significant departure in government policy and signals that greater involvement of primary care professionals in the planning and delivery of care is not negotiable. Of equal significance is the collective ethos with which PCG/Ts are imbued. Decision-making is undertaken by the PCG board or PCT executive committee (ratified by the PCT board) and the results are applied throughout the group. The PCG/T also has a clearly defined corporate responsibility for monitoring and assuring the quality of clinical services provided by constituent members via clinical governance (discussed further in Chapter 3). In a very real sense, primary care professionals have become their brother's keepers – a stark contrast to the highly fragmented and autonomous culture that has hitherto characterised primary care.

An extended remit for commissioning

The commissioning responsibilities of primary care professionals have been considerably enhanced in contrast to GP fundholding and even 'total' purchasing. PCG/Ts have been endowed with 'unified budgets' that comprise the majority of local NHS spending (significantly, for the first time the entire community prescribing budget is subject to a local cash limit). PCG/Ts have also been given expanded commissioning responsibilities that go beyond the traditional boundary of the practice population. A key role now is to identify the broader health needs within the local community (and, in particular, any existing inequalities in health or health services) and to put in place a plan to address them.

Previous models of GP commissioning involved an accountability arrangement between primary care and 'others' (most obviously hospital services providers). Significantly, PCTs may now commission primary medical services, in addition to specialist and community care, through personal medical services (PMS) pilots (discussed further below). Thus, GP-led organisations will increasingly act as the prime accountable agent for GPs themselves. This introduces interesting conflicts of interest and represents a blurring of managerial accountability and professional self-regulation.

An erosion of the purchaser–provider split

While the language of the internal market has been abandoned, many of its principles and structures have been retained, not least the 'purchaser–provider split' in relation to specialist hospital services. However, this separation has been abandoned in relation to the provision of community, rehabilitation and, in some cases, specialist mental health service. Level four PCTs are able to purchase *and* provide these services as part of a strategy to encourage cost- and clinically-effective care substitution, and better integration between general practice and community health services. In effect, primary care professionals within a PCT can use their commissioning powers to reward themselves for extended service provision.

What does the early research evidence tell us about PCGs and their emerging accountability? Clearly, PCGs are developing as organisations at distinctly different speeds. Many PCGs appear to have made good progress in establishing an infrastructure for clinical governance and in setting minimum standards for constituent general practices. Therefore, the 'collectivisation' objective has been supported by practical achievements in the early days of PCGs. However, less encouragingly (from the Government's perspective at least), PCGs have devoted little time to addressing wider health improvement issues of their communities, and many PCGs lack the information and management capacity required for rigorous budget management and planning.[9]

Primary care provision

PCG/Ts have inherited from health authorities (and, before them, family health services authorities) the responsibility for 'developing' primary care. To date, this developmental activity has been largely voluntary and exhortative. In fact, local health agencies have had few opportunities to influence the provision of general medical services (GMS) within their locality. The formal contract that has governed the funding and provision of GMS is a national one (negotiated by the Department of Health and representatives of the British Medical Association) and has been characterised by the substantial latitude it allows individual GPs to be masters of their own destiny, free from local direction or restriction. The provision of GP services has been the NHS sector that has hitherto demonstrated the greatest policy stability,[8] notwithstanding the seismic shock in 1990 when new contract terms were unilaterally imposed upon an unwilling profession.[11]

In this policy arena, the in-coming Labour government inherited changes to the organisational and contractual framework within which primary medical services were to be provided, in the shape of personal medical services (PMS) pilots (similar pilots were also introduced for general dental services). These pilots, often dubbed a 'silent revolution', look set to transform the relationship between State and general practice. Pilots share a number of key characteristics:

- They replace the national GP contract with the Secretary of State for Health with a local contract held by either a health authority or a PCT.
- The specification and cost of the service provided (including GP remuneration) are negotiated locally.
- The PMS contract is monitored and 'performance managed' locally.
- New opportunities for the salaried employment of GPs are introduced.

PMS pilots are bringing profound changes to the nature of the accountability of general practice. Organised medical interests at national level (the General Practice Committee of the British Medical Association) no longer enjoys a monopoly over the negotiation with government to set terms and conditions. At a stroke, the collective bargaining that has characterised GP–governmental relations has been undermined. Indeed, with PMS pilots heralding medical services led by NHS trusts and even independent contractor nurses, the monopoly of GPs themselves in providing these services has been broken. Perhaps unsurprisingly, the introduction of PMS pilots brought forth noticeable opposition from some quarters of general practice.[12]

From apparently only lukewarm support for PMS pilots, the Government has increasingly brought them centre stage. *The NHS Plan* announced that a majority of GPs were expected to enter PMS by 2004, that existing pilots could become permanent, and even that single-handed GPs may be forced to enter the PMS scheme. Even without the threat of compulsion, PMS pilots have increased in number rapidly over the three 'waves' (see Table 5.1). Within three years of the Government's tenure, the national GP contract, so long the hallmark of NHS primary care, looks increasingly endangered and obsolete. Significantly, *The NHS Plan* also indicated the Government's commitment to overhauling the GMS contract. Convergence between PMS and GMS appears imminent.

Table 5.1: Numbers of pilots by wave

Pilot type	Wave 1	Wave 2	Wave 3
Trust based	26	22	
Practice based	53	179	
Other/Not known	4	2	1231
Total	83	203	1231*

* Figures based on approved applications

As PMS pilots proliferate, the relationship between GPs and the NHS is increasingly being mediated through local health bodies rather than through national negotiation with government. Local contracts offer an opportunity to specify in precise terms the mutual expectations of contract 'principal' and 'agent'. They also provide means to exact compliance (something that remains deficient under GMS given the 'broad brush' nature of the national contract terms). This far more intimate relationship suggests that the ability to hold general practice to account has increased.

In fact, early evidence is more equivocal. Health authorities are regularly reviewing pilots.[13] However, while first wave contracts have been characterised by their diversity, few have included terms that are either specific or onerous.[7,14] This may be set to change. Third wave PMS pilots face a mandatory national contractual framework that must form the basis of their 'local' contract (see Table 5.2). This framework incorporates a range of expectations that are far in advance of those demanded under GMS (at least as currently formulated). After two waves of pilots characterised by diversity and autonomy (a 'thousand flowers blooming'), future pilots look set to be reined in more purposefully by the centre. The Government's determination to achieve greater responsiveness from general practice appears clear; although, to date, relatively low priority has been given by pilots to developing accountable relationships directly with patients.[13]

A new apparatus for central control

The Labour government's primary care policy is a curious mix of centralisation and decentralisation.[15] On the one hand, PCG/Ts have been devolved significant powers and responsibilities to commission and provide services. In addition, the GP and general dental (and soon community pharmacy) contracts have apparently been handed to local agencies to determine funding, activity and accountability arrangements. *The NHS Plan* promises to reward those organisations that perform well with 'earned autonomy' and freedom from interference from above.

At the same time, the Government has created a potentially fearsome machinery for central control. A burgeoning industry in national service frameworks is setting out a template for service delivery that must be applied throughout the NHS – the requirements of primary care are specific and onerous. The National Institute for Clinical Excellence is producing national guidelines and the Commission for Health Improvement will assess the implementation of clinical governance and investigate unsatisfactory performance at all levels within the NHS. *The NHS Plan* also announces a raft of new 'task-forces' – centrally mandated groups that will oversee the implementation of the Plan. 'Earned autonomy' may translate as the freedom to do as one is told.[16]

Table 5.2: Key features of the contractual framework for PMS pilots – Third wave

• Achievement of national service framework requirements and national cancer guidelines.
• Compliance with local HImP targets.
• Completion of three audits annually.
• Achievement of 'higher' GMS targets for immunisation and cervical cytology.
• Patients able to see clinician within 24 hours, and GP within 48 hours.
• Compliance with NHS human resource policies and implementation of the NHS staff appraisal system.
• Introduction of national guidelines for reporting adverse care events.
• Submission to external financial audit.
• GPs to spend a minimum of 30 hours per year on continuing professional development.
• Completion of annual report.

Systems of accountability require information as their life-blood. The Labour government has begun to address the long-standing deficit in both accurate data and meaningful information. A new performance assessment framework (PAF)

was introduced in 1999 and new indicators continue to be developed. The PAF will now apply to PCTs providing community services, and the Commission for Health Improvement and the Audit Commission are jointly tasked to publish results for each trust annually. Significantly, more comparative information is to be demanded of primary care. From 2001, every GP practice and PCG/T will monitor GP referral rates to specialist services. Increasingly, primary care can expect its own performance to be assessed and reported in the public domain.

Conclusion – A new accountability for primary care?

The balance between centre and periphery continues to shift in complex ways, and accountability relationships are being redefined as a consequence. What are the implications for the accountability of primary care?

There seems little doubt that the Government has used its recent injection of resources into the NHS and the growing public disquiet over the apparently poor regulation of professionals to renegotiate the relationship between doctors and the State. Much of this attention has focused on primary care, not least because it is here that ministers hope that the holy grail of 'demand management' might be located (in particular, ending the annual debacle of 'winter pressures'). This has continued the trend established by previous Conservative governments, stretching back to 1990 if not before.

Professional accountability – the holding to account only by one's peers – has increased through the creation of PCG/Ts. These organisations are founded on the collaboration of primary care clinicians in carrying out policy-making and management responsibilities. PCG/Ts have a core remit, among other things, to examine the clinical performance of constituents. Managerial accountability, too, has increased. PCGs are located firmly within the NHS management hierarchy – regional directors of the NHS will sign off PCT performance reports and the personal development plans and performance-related pay of PCT chief executives. What of political accountability? Here the picture is more cloudy. PCG/Ts are mandated to represent and involve their population. They include local people on their boards and often in other structures below board level. PCG/Ts, therefore, are expected to be politically accountable to 'the people', although it is far from clear how this process might be successfully managed. PCTs, by linking formally with elected local authorities, are likely to make this tension between managerial and political accountability more overt.

Have the 'corporate rationalisers' stolen a march on the 'medical monopolists'?[17] It would be an over-simplification to suggest that primary care has now come within the grip of central NHS management. Under Labour, primary care has greater sway over the planning and delivery of health services than ever before. Yet they now have to contend with an accountability framework that is more explicit, and more top-down than before. The price of power is accountability.

The accountability framework for primary care is significantly different under Labour (see Table 5.3).

Should PMS be seen as a counterfoil to the centralising trends of New Labour? After all, PMS appears to be leading to the dismantling of the national GMS contract and formal collective bargaining between government and the BMA. The announcement in *The NHS Plan* of a new system of local resource allocation, including all of GMS, would appear to make the demise of the GMS contract inevitable. Thus, it might be argued that primary care, in its role as health *commissioner*, has been held increasingly accountable to managers and to the centre. In contrast, in its role as service *provider*, primary care is experiencing a trend towards greater decentralisation and autonomy. Whether this persists is another matter. The contracts for third wave PMS pilots look rather different to the diversity created in the first two waves. The convergence between PMS and GMS may well result in a new model national contract (albeit with more local discretion at the edges).

Table 5.3 Primary care accountability compared

Pre-Labour NHS	*New NHS* under Labour
Based on acts/omissions of the individual	Collective responsibility for acts/omissions of individuals
Primarily self-/ professionally-regulated	External regulation of professions (e.g. CHI)
Separation between financial and clinical accountability	Financial and clinical accountability unified within PCG/T
Less structured agenda for public involvement/ accountability in primary care	Overt agenda for public involvement/ accountability in primary care

If a fundamental requirement of accountability is the existence of an agreed language about conduct and performance,[18] then *The NHS Plan*, the performance assessment framework and the welter of national guidelines provide this for primary care (and indeed the rest of the NHS). Whether the means to exact compliance and control exist is another matter altogether. General practice has proved successful in the past in eluding the embrace of government or management – this may yet be the case in the future.

References

[1] Mulgan R. 'Accountability': an ever-expanding concept? *Public Administration* 2000; (78) 3: 555–73.

[2] De Roo A, Maarse H. Understanding the central–local relationship in health care: a new approach. *International Journal of Health Planning and Management* 1990; 5: 15–25.

[3] Klein R. *The new politics of the NHS.* 3rd ed. London: Longman, 1995.

[4] Paton C. Devolution and centralism in the NHS. *Social Policy and Administration* 1993; 27 (2); 83–108.

[5] Packwood T, Keen J, Buxton M. *Hospitals in transition: the resource management experience.* Milton Keynes: Open University Press, 1991.

[6] Mays N, Mulligan J, Goodwin N. The British quasi-market in health care: a balance sheet of the evidence. *Journal of Health Services Research and Policy* 2000; 5 (1): 49–58.

[7] Lewis R, Malbon G, Gillam S. A future for primary care groups? In: *Health Care UK 1999/2000.* London: King's Fund, 1999: 9–14.

[8] NHS Executive. *Primary care trusts – establishing better services.* London: NHS Executive, 1999.

[9] Wilkin D, Gillam S, Leese B, editors. *The national tracker survey of primary care groups and trusts – progress and challenges 1999/2000.* Manchester: NPCRDC/King's Fund,

1999.

[10] Lewis R, Mays N. Trends in government health policy – from GMS to PMS. In: Lewis R, Gillam S, editors. *Transforming primary care – personal medical services in the new NHS.* London: King's Fund, 1999.

[11] Day P. The state, the NHS and general practice. *Journal of Public Health Policy* 1992; 13 (2): 165–79.

[12] Jenkins C. Personal medical services pilots – new opportunities. In: Lewis R, Gillam S, editors. *Transforming primary care – personal medical services in the new NHS.* London: King's Fund, 1999.

[13] Walsh N, Andre C, Barnes M, Huntington J, Rogers H, Baines D. Accountability, integration and responsiveness. In: *National evaluation of first wave NHS personal medical services pilots: integrated interim report from four research projects.* Manchester: NPCRDC, 2000.

[14] Sheaff R, Lloyd-Kendall A. Principal–agent relationships in general practice: the first wave of English PMS pilot contracts. *Journal of Health Services Research and Policy* 2000; 5 (3): 156–63.

[15] Lewis R, Gillam S, Gosden T, Sheaff R. Who contracts for primary care? *Journal of Public Health Medicine* 1999; 21 (4): 367–72.

[16] Lewis R. How national a health service. *Health Matters* 2000; 40: 6–7.

[17] Lewis R, Gillam S. The National Health Service Plan: further reform of British health care. *International Journal of Health Services* 2001; 31 (1): 111–18.

[18] Alford R R. *Health care politics.* Chicago: University of Chicago Press, 1975.

[19] Day P, Klein R. *Accountabilities: five public services.* London: Tavistock Publications, 1987.

Chapter 6: Beyond *The NHS Plan*

Stephen Gillam

A new NHS?

What are the prospects for primary care as we contemplate this government's potential second term? Certainly, the new investment should do much to address Britain's hitherto parsimonious record on health spending. Any complacency that Britain was somehow continuing to get a quart out of a pint pot was dispelled by the World Health Organisation's recent ranking of health systems.[1] The UK was well outside the premier division. The aim of *The NHS Plan* is to deliver swift access to comprehensive care bearing any international comparison, while maintaining the structure of the NHS and universal coverage. Whether this can be achieved at a cost that is sustainable without alternative forms of finance remains to be seen. Other questions remain.

Will access be improved?

The expansion in hospital beds and consultant numbers with consequent reductions in waiting times, if realised, will ease the burden of containment in primary care. The expansion in GP numbers is less impressive. Even allowing for investment in other community-based services, an extra 2000 GPs will not easily be able to improve access to their services or extend consultation lengths. Longer term, the expansion of medical school places offers better GP recruitment prospects than face planners for the critically important nursing workforce.

Moves to integrate NHS Direct and GP out-of-hours services make sense. The vision is of a single phone call to NHS Direct as the one-stop gateway to all out-of-hours health care but, as Dominique Florin implies, we do not know if this is really what users want.

More contentiously, it is possible that intermediate care will follow the same trajectory as long-term care in the 1980s.[2] With their devolved, unified budgets, PCTs assume new financial risks. Because they can levy charges for personal care, PCTs will have clear incentives to shift intermediate care into non-NHS settings. The funding mechanisms governing payment of providers will be critical. Experience in other countries indicates that moves towards risk-adjusted capitation payments typical of voluntary insurance may, without careful regulation, expose the public to poor quality care in the private sector.[3]

What are the prospects for dentistry?

The Prime Minister will be unable to keep his promise to provide for everyone who wants access to NHS dentistry by the end of 2001. The dental strategy does not significantly expand NHS capacity. There are few financial incentives to attract dentists back into the NHS. How can they be encouraged to do more NHS work? The Government sets NHS fees, in discussion with the dental profession, and could if it wished increase their fees tomorrow. Perversely, the drive to improve the standards of NHS dental services could even make the problem worse. For some dentists, the prospect of a 'modernised' service, performance managed by the Department of Health, could provide a further incentive to go into the private sector, where there is more time for each patient and little scrutiny. For dentists able to access a market, private practice is as attractive an option now as it has ever been, and while this is true the capacity of NHS dentistry to deliver a service that is truly accessible to all will remain compromised.

Rather than focus on the NHS, the Government could have created policies for the dental profession as a whole. *The NHS Plan* proposes 'concordats' with the medical profession for elective surgery and other services. Could there not be a concordat for dentistry? The concordat could, among other things, set targets for access to dental services that all dentists would be required to meet.[4]

Oddly, the Government's dental strategy does not appear to acknowledge that general dental services now operate in a market. In more affluent areas, many dentists offer both NHS and private care. Patients can therefore choose to buy private dentistry – where it is available – if they can afford the price, and believe they will receive a high quality of care. This vision haunts those who foresee GP secession from the NHS should their payment mechanisms be similarly destabilised.

Will these investments increase efficiency?
Increasingly, patients who currently go to hospital will be able to have tests and treatment in one of 500 new primary care centres. Consultants who previously worked only in hospitals will be seeing out-patients in these settings, while specialist GPs will be taking referrals from their colleagues in fields such as ophthalmology, orthopaedics and dermatology. The model for these is untested. Evidence suggests that outreach clinics and minor injury units' work are low volume and cost

inefficient.[5] Similarly, the investment in intermediate care represents something of a triumph of ideology over evidence. Services both to facilitate and to prevent hospital admissions have the potential to improve the quality of life of older people, but they can easily silt up if not carefully targeted.

After nearly a decade of rhetoric in support of the 'primary care-led NHS', there is little evidence of a shift in the balance of NHS expenditure. In absolute terms it is the acute sector that continues to attract most new money.[6] Will PCTs have the critical mass they need to lever resources from hospitals into community-based services? In many areas, PCG mergers give PCTs the aura and scale of the health authorities they replaced. One fear is that they will fossilise as their bureaucracies burgeon, rather than develop the agility needed for efficient commissioning.

Will these proposals improve clinical care?

The clinical governance initiative is welcome. It should improve clinical standards in absolute terms but could conceivably widen variations between practices in different parts of the country. In areas where there is a history of joint working and inter-practice audit has been embedded, progress on implementation is already apparent. In other areas, as Rebecca Rosen suggests, primary care professionals are still groping to understand the meaning of the term and little visible has changed. This underlines the importance of moving forward today's revalidation proposals and reforms to the processes of professional self-regulation. The loss of struggling colleagues and the time out needed to participate in continuing professional development will increase workloads, and it remains to be seen whether these changes will do enough to reassure the public. The refurbishment of 3000 practices should, of course, improve the quality of inner city care.

Though 'quality-based contracts' are hard to devise, local contracting under PMS ought to effect quality improvements.[7] Early comparisons between first wave PMS and GMS practices give limited grounds for optimism,[8] but extra leverage will be available to PCTs working with succeeding waves.

Does *The NHS Plan* narrow the 'democratic deficit' that has plagued the NHS since its inception?

Will Anderson is not alone in viewing the proposed structural changes with some scepticism. In the 'new NHS', the role of patients is confirmed as that of 'consumers' rather than as citizens/stakeholders. Central agencies will have patient representatives, but which constituency they represent is still unclear. On the other hand, the new role for elected local government in scrutinising the work of NHS bodies represents a potentially important counterbalance. This may make centralisation more difficult to achieve.

Can primary care play a leading role in improving population health?

Previous attempts to sell the 'public health function' to primary care professionals have foundered. For the most part, they have neither the time, skills nor inclination to lead this work, although primary care nurses, particularly health visitors, could be equipped to spearhead this role. Progress on partnership building at the level of the PCG/T is as yet patchy. The jury is out on whether these organisations can really work effectively beyond the health service to tackle the determinants of health inequalities.

Does *The NHS Plan* represent further centralisation of British health policy?

Richard Lewis characterises the first three years of the Labour government's administration in terms of an ambiguous mix of centralism and devolution.[9] At first sight, these latest proposals are couched in a vocabulary suggesting local discretion. In reality, *The NHS Plan* tightens central control. Whatever the Government's intentions, NHS clinicians and managers will soon operate within an environment that is dominated by pre-determined clinical frameworks and an enhanced performance management framework. Hence the importance of the PMS initiative as a pressure valve allowing local self-determination.

Much, of course, depends on the manner of *The NHS Plan*'s implementation. Recent history has underlined how important it is to defuse the opposition to change of organised medicine.[10] The Plan itself bears the signatures of no fewer than 25 leaders of professional associations, trades unions and pressure groups. Whether the Government has won the hearts and minds of the rank and file is another matter. On the one hand, most health service employees appreciate that such governmental largesse is unlikely ever to be repeated. On the other hand, many are cynical after years of costly restructuring that have been of no apparent benefit to patients. The BMA leadership was driven to tone down its initial support for the Plan to tune in with a disgruntled membership.

A new professionalism?

Many general practitioners hark back to a 'golden age' in the '70s and '80s following the *Family Practice Charter* of 1966.

Primary health care teams were steadily expanding and their status was rising. While seeming to endorse an expanded role in distributing resources, this government has at the same time hacked into some of the most fundamental sources of their power and influence. The gate-keeping role of GPs that emerged with their rights of referral to charitable hospitals in the nineteenth century is seen as monopolistic. As other routes of access to care open up, traditional referral arrangements will seem increasingly restrictive.

For those of an apocalyptic disposition, general practice is ever on the edge of revolutionary change. The collectivisation of primary care under Labour marks a move toward managed care under UK-style health maintenance organisations. The PMS initiative heralds the end of the national contract and changes the nature of independent contractor status. Generalist care is no longer to be provided by individual practitioners but from inter-professional units under local contracts. As today's surgeries increasingly become the service output for a larger primary care organisation, many 'corner shops' will disappear.

Demographic and other pressures on the primary care workforce carry their own imperatives. Persisting nurse shortages and the retirement of a cadre of overseas-trained general practitioners serving inner city populations determine the need for new networks of provision. Both within and out-of-hours, a plurality of nurse-led providers will form the first point of contact. In many respects, nurses *are* the future of primary care, but a feminised, increasingly part-time GP work force will happily accede to more flexible working arrangements. Could the emergence of many more salaried non-principals create a new form of 'two-tierism' with less well-remunerated, peripatetic doctors providing more care in deprived areas? Or will these changes mean that personal care in the traditional sense may be restricted to those with complex chronic diseases – from their specialist GP or community consultant – or for those private patients able to pay for extras?

Conclusion

Such visions are prematurely pessimistic. The emergence of powerful GP managers and medical directors need not be accompanied by the relegation of their traditional caring roles. History suggests that health service users will continue to place a premium on these ever scarcer traditional virtues – and there is no reason to suppose that nurses cannot provide them as well as doctors. The trade-off implied between personal continuity and modern care can be exaggerated. A greater challenge both to the new primary care organisations and to the health workers within them is to meet the varying needs and demands of service users for the information they need to share decision-making. Far from depersonalising clinical practice, the information revolution can help change doctors and nurses from being repositories of knowledge to being managers of knowledge.[11] Creative use of IT, particularly the Internet to communicate with patients, will be central to future clinical practice. Fundamental redesign rather than ever-faster spinning of the 'hamster wheel' of health care is likely to be the only way to sustain the NHS and those working within it.[12]

Apothecaries and barber surgeons began working from their 'surgeries' nearly 200 years ago. Their descendants are reclaiming surgical skills, and the ambitious investment programme for NHS Lift suggests that pronouncements on the death of the surgery may be premature. Practices are likely to remain the basic building block for the time being. A single electronic record will, in time, offer exciting opportunities to integrate information from different providers and to support more self-care from home. PCTs offer an administrative and organisational model to support service integration, for example out of hours, more cost effectively. PCTs offer not the gulag but opportunities for virtual integration (across networks of primary care professionals) and vertical integration (with colleagues in secondary care) around which to expand community-based services – a prerequisite of 'fundamental redesign'.

The cost efficiency of the NHS has long been attributed in large measure to the strengths of British general practice, a key feature of which is a comprehensive financing system. There are risks in unravelling the national contract for GPs, but potential gains too. Top-down governance is acknowledged as having failed to provide the innovation and the responsiveness to deliver sustained improvement in patient care. The third way of a new post-PMS contract could yet liberate the local entrepreneurs. For the gains of the last 30 years will not be easily be swept away. History suggests that politicians and policy-makers easily underestimate the power of professionals and their representative institutions. Primary care practitioners should look forward with cautious optimism as a likely Labour government attempts to fill the other half of the glass over the next five years. Some of the heat has passed out of debates over rationing and long-term funding of the NHS – temporarily. In terms of its targets, *The NHS Plan* will surely fail, but this administration has earned the right to count 'the last throw of the state monopoly dice'.

References

1 World Health Organisation. *Health systems: improving performance.* Geneva: WHO, 2000.

2 Pollock A. Will intermediate care be the undoing of the NHS? *BMJ* 2000; 321: 393–94.

3 Fine J, Chalmers J. 'User pays' and other approaches to funding long term care for older people in Australia. *Ageing and Society* 2000; 20: 5–32.

4 Keen, J. (Personal communication).

5 Shapiro J, Roland M, editors. *Outreach clinics.* Oxford: Radcliffe Press, 1996.

6 Gillam S. Homeward bound? Just how far have we come in re-directing resources to primary care? *Health Management* 2000; November: 14–15.

7 Lewis R, Gillam S, Gosden T, Sheaff R. Who contracts for primary care? *J. Public Health Med.* 1999; 21: 367–71.

8 The National PMS Evaluation Team. *National evaluation of first wave NHS personal medical services pilots: integrated interim report from four research projects.* Manchester: National Primary Care Research and Development Centre, 2000.

9 Lewis, R. How national a health service? *Health Matters* 2000; 40: 6–7.

10 Ham C. *The politics of NHS reform, 1988–97. Metaphor or*